Will looked to the right. Then to the left.

He brushed the stinging snow out of his eyes but he couldn't see the other sleds. He looked behind. They were straggling along, twenty and now thirty feet in back of him. The new sled skimmed along, the runners singing happily. Both Will and Orv felt a strange thrill of excitement.

Usually when the sleds reached the bottom of the hill they slowed down abruptly and stopped. But not this sled. It kept on; its momentum carried it on and on a hundred yards farther than any of the other sleds had ever reached.

"We flew down the hill, Orv," Will said breathlessly.

"We flew," Orv repeated.

THE WRIGHT BROTHERS

PIONEERS OF AMERICAN AVIATION

BY QUENTIN REYNOLDS

Landmark Books®

Random House New York

Copyright © 1950 by Random House, Inc. Copyright renewed 1978 by James J. Reynolds and Frederick H. Rohlfs, Esq., and Random House, Inc. All rights reserved under International and Pan-American Copyright Conventions. Published in the United States by Random House Children's Books, a division of Random House, Inc., New York, and simultaneously in Canada by Random House of Canada Limited, Toronto. Originally published by Random House, Inc., in 1950.

www.randomhouse.com/kids

Cover photograph of the Wright airplane in France, 1908, with pilot Wilbur Wright and a pupil courtesy of North Wind Picture Archives.

Library of Congress Cataloging-in-Publication Data
Reynolds, Quentin James. The Wright brothers, pioneers of American aviation.
(Landmark books)
SUMMARY: A biography of the two brothers from Dayton, Ohio, who built and flew the first airplane.
1. Wright, Orville, 1871–1948—Juvenile literature. 2. Wright, Wilbur, 1867–1912—Juvenile literature. 3. Aeronautics—United States—Biography—Juvenile literature. [1. Wright, Orville, 1871–1948. 2. Wright, Wilbur, 1867–1912. 3. Aeronautics—Biography.] I. Title.
TL540.W7R48 1981 629.13'092'2 [B] [920] 80-23605
ISBN 0-394-84700-8

Printed in the United States of America 41
RANDOM HOUSE and colophon and LANDMARK BOOKS and colophon are registered trademarks of Random House, Inc.

Contents

1

Learning from Mother

Susan Wright wasn't like other mothers.

She was younger and prettier than most other mothers, and she liked to laugh and she liked to play games with her three youngest children: Wilbur, who was eleven; Orville, who was seven; and Katharine, who was four.

The other mothers would shake their heads and say, "Susan Wright spoils those children; lets 'em do anything they want. No good will come of it."

But Susan Wright only laughed. In the summer she'd pack a picnic lunch and she, the two boys, and little Kate (no one ever called her Katharine) would go and spend a day in the woods. Mrs. Wright knew the name of every bird and she could tell a bird by his song. Wilbur and Orville learned to tell birds too.

One day they sat on the banks of a river near Dayton, where they lived. Wilbur and Orville were fishing. Everyone called Wilbur "Will," and of course Orville was "Orv." The fish weren't biting very well. Suddenly a big bird swooped down, stuck his long bill into the river, came out with a tiny fish, and then swooped right up into the sky again.

"What makes a bird fly, Mother?" Wilbur asked.

"Their wings, Will," she said. "You notice they move their wings and that makes them go faster."

"But Mother," Will said, not quite satisfied, "that bird that just swooped down didn't even move his wings. He swooped down, grabbed a fish, and then went right up again. He never moved his wings at all."

"The wind doesn't just blow *toward* you or *away* from you," she said. "It blows *up* and *down* too. When a current of air blows up, it takes the bird up. His wings support him in the air."

"If we had wings, then we could fly too, couldn't we, Mother?" Wilbur asked.

"But God didn't give us wings." She laughed.

"Maybe we could make wings," Wilbur insisted.

"Maybe," his mother said thoughtfully. "But I don't know. No one ever did make wings that would allow a boy to fly."

"I will someday," Wilbur said, and Orville nodded and said, "I will too."

"Well, when you're a little older maybe you can try," their mother said.

That was another thing about Susan Wright. Most other mothers would have thought that this was foolish talk. Most other mothers would have said, "Oh, don't be silly, who ever heard of such nonsense!" But not Susan Wright. She knew that even an eleven-year-old boy can have ideas of his own, and just because they happened to come from an eleven-year-old head—well, that didn't make them foolish. She never treated her children as if they were babies, and perhaps that's why they liked to go fishing with her or on picnics with her. And that's why they kept asking her questions.

She always gave them sensible answers.

They asked their father questions too, but he was a traveling minister and he was away a lot.

"It's getting chilly," Mrs. Wright said suddenly. "Look at those gray clouds, Will."

Wilbur looked up. "It's going to snow, I bet," he said happily.

"No more picnics until next spring," his mother said. "Yes, it looks like snow. We'd better be getting home."

As they reached home, the first big white snowflakes started to fall. They kept falling all that night and all the next day. It was the first real snowstorm of the year.

In the morning the wind was blowing so fiercely that Wilbur found it hard to walk to the barn where the wood was stored. The wind was so strong it almost knocked him down. He burst through the kitchen door with an armful of wood for the stove, and he told his mother about the wind.

"The thing to do is to lean forward into the wind," she said. "Bend over, and that way you get closer to the ground and you get under the wind."

That night when Wilbur had to make the

trip for more wood, he tried his mother's idea. To his surprise, it worked! When he was bent over, the wind didn't seem nearly so strong.

After a few days the wind stopped, and now the whole countryside was covered with snow. Wilbur and Orville, with little Kate trailing behind, hurried to the Big Hill not far from the house.

Orville's schoolmates were all there with their sleds. It was a good hill to coast down because no roads came anywhere near it, and even if they had, it wouldn't have mattered. This was 1878 and there were no automobiles. Horse-drawn sleighs traveled the roads in winter. The horses had bells fastened to their collars. As they jogged along, the bells rang and you could hear them a mile away.

Most of the boys had their own sleds; not the kind boys have now, but old-fashioned sleds with two wooden runners. No one ever thought of owning a "bought" sled. In those days a boy's father made a sled for him.

The boys who had sleds of their own let Wilbur and Orville ride down the hill with them. Ed Sines and Chauncey Smith and Johnny Morrow and Al Johnston all owned sleds, but they liked to race one another down the long hill. When this happened, Wilbur and Orville just had to stand there and watch. Late that afternoon the boys came home, with Kate behind them, and their mother noticed that they were very quiet. She soon found out why they were unhappy.

"Why doesn't Father build us a sled?" Wilbur blurted out.

"But Father is away, Will," his mother said gently. "And you know how busy he is when he is at home. He has to write stories for the church paper and he has to write sermons. Now suppose we build a sled together."

Wilbur laughed. "Whoever heard of anyone's mother building a sled?"

"You just wait," his mother said. "We'll build a better sled than Ed Sines has. Now get me a pencil and a piece of paper."

"You goin' to build a sled out of paper?" Orville asked in amazement.

"Just wait," she repeated.

2

"Get It Right on Paper"

Will and Orv brought their mother a pencil and paper, and she went to the minister's desk and found a ruler. Then she sat down at the kitchen table. "First we'll draw a picture of the sled," she said.

"What good is a picture of a sled?" Orville asked.

"Now Orville, watch Mother." She picked up the ruler in one hand and the pencil in the other.

"We want one like Ed Sines has," Orville said.

"When you go coasting, how many boys will Ed Sines's sled hold?" she asked.

"Two," Wilbur said.

"We'll make this one big enough to hold three," she said. "Maybe you can take Kate along sometimes." The outline of a sled began to appear on the paper. As she drew it she talked. "You see, Ed's sled is about four feet long. I've seen it often enough. We'll make this one five feet long. Now, Ed's sled is about a foot off the ground, isn't it?"

Orville nodded, his eyes never leaving the drawing that was taking shape. It was beginning to look like a sled now, but not like the sleds the other boys had.

"You've made it too low," Will said.

"You want a sled that's faster than Ed's sled, don't you?" His mother smiled. "Well, Ed's sled is at least a foot high. Our sled will be lower—closer to the ground. It won't meet so much wind resistance."

"Wind resistance?" It was the first time Wilbur had ever heard the expression. He looked blankly at his mother.

"Remember the blizzard last week?" she asked. "Remember when you went out to the woodshed and the wind was so strong you could hardly walk to the shed? I told you to lean over, and on the next trip to the woodshed you did. When you came back with an armful of wood you laughed and said, 'Mother, I leaned 'way forward and got under the wind.' You were closer to the ground and you were able to lessen the wind resistance. Now, the closer to the ground our sled is, the less wind resistance there will be, and the faster it will go."

"Wind resistance . . . wind resistance," Wilbur repeated, and maybe the airplane was born in that moment. Certainly neither Will nor Orville Wright ever forgot that first lesson in speed.

"How do you know about these things, Mother?" Wilbur asked.

"You'd be surprised how much mothers know, Will." She laughed. She didn't tell the boys that when she was a little girl at school her best subject had been arithmetic. It just came naturally to her. It was the same when she went to high school. And when she went to college, algebra and geometry were her best subjects. That was why she knew all about things like wind resistance.

Finally she finished the drawing. The boys leaned over the table to look at it. This sled was going to be longer than Ed's sled and much narrower. Ed's sled was about three feet wide. This one looked as if it would be only half that wide.

"You made it narrow," Wilbur said shrewdly, "to make it faster. The narrower it is, the less wind resistance."

"That's right." His mother nodded. "Now let's put down the exact length of the runners and the exact width of the sled."

"But that's only a paper sled," Orville protested.

"If you get it right on paper," she said calmly, "it'll be right when you build it. Always remember that."

" 'If you get it right on paper, it'll be right when you build it,' " Wilbur repeated, and his mother looked at him sharply. Sometimes Will seemed older than his eleven years. Little Orville was quick to give you an answer to anything, but as often as not he'd forget the answer right away. When Will learned something he never forgot it.

"Mother, you make all your clothes," Wilbur said thoughtfully. "You always make a drawing first."

"We call that the pattern," his mother said. "I draw and then cut out a pattern that's exactly the size of the dress I am going to make. And . . ."

"If the pattern is right, it'll be right when you make the dress," he finished. She nodded.

"Now you two boys get started on your sled." She smiled. "There are plenty of planks out in the barn. Find the very lightest ones. Don't use planks with knots in them. You saw the planks to the right size, Will—don't let Orville touch the saw."

"May we use Father's tools?" Wilbur asked breathlessly.

His mother nodded. "I don't think your father will mind. I know you'll be careful with them. Just follow the drawing exactly," she warned once more.

The two boys and Kate hurried out to the barn. They realized that this was an important occasion. Wilbur always chopped the wood for the stove when his father was away, but he had never been allowed to use the gleaming tools that lay in his father's tool chest.

Three days later their sled was finished. They pulled it out of the barn and asked their mother to inspect it. She had her tape measure with her and she measured it. The runners were exactly the length she had put down in her drawing. In fact, the boys had followed every direction she had given them. The runners gleamed. Orville had polished them with sandpaper until they were as smooth as silk.

"We thought of one other thing, Mother," Will said. "We found some old candles in the woodshed. We rubbed the runners with the candles. See how smooth they are?"

Mrs. Wright nodded. She had forgotten to tell the boys that, but they'd thought it out for themselves. "Now try your sled," she told them.

Followed by Kate, the boys dragged their new sled to the hill only half a mile away where their pals were coasting. They looked at the new sled in amazement. It was long and very narrow. It looked as though it wouldn't hold anyone. The runners were thin compared to those on their own sleds.

"Who made that for you?" Ed Sines asked.

"Mother showed us how," Wilbur said proudly. Some of the boys laughed. Whoever heard of a boy's mother knowing how to make a sled?

"It looks as if it would fall apart if you sat on it," Al Johnston said, and he laughed too.

"Come on, we'll race you down the hill," another cried out.

"All right, two on each sled," Wilbur said. He wasn't a bit afraid. He was sure the drawing had been right, and because he and Orv had followed the drawing, he knew that the sled was right.

They lined the four sleds up. Will and Orv sat on their sled, but it didn't "fall apart." Suddenly Wilbur got an idea.

"Get up, Orv," he said. "Now lie down on the sled . . . that's it . . . spread your legs a bit." Will then flopped down on top of his brother. "Less wind resistance this way," he whispered.

"Give us all a push," Ed Sines yelled.

And then they were off. It was an even start. The four sleds gathered speed, for at the top the slope was steep. Will looked to the right. Then to the left. He brushed the stinging snow out of his eyes but he couldn't see the other sleds. He looked behind. They were straggling along, twenty and now thirty feet in back of him. The new sled skimmed along, the runners singing happily. Both Will and Orv felt a strange thrill of excitement. They approached the bottom of the long hill. The other sleds were far, far behind now.

Usually when the sleds reached the bottom of the hill they slowed down abruptly and stopped. But not this sled. It kept on; its momentum carried it on and on a hundred yards farther than any of the other sleds had ever reached. Finally it stopped.

Shaking with excitement, Will and Orv stood up.

"We flew down the hill, Orv," Will said breathlessly.

"We flew," Orv repeated.

Now Ed and Al and Johnny ran up, excited at what had happened. No sled had gone so far or so fast as the one Will and Orv had built.

"You *flew* down the hill," Ed Sines gasped. "Let me try it?"

Wilbur looked at Orv, and some secret message seemed to pass between them. They had built this sled together, and it was the best sled there was. They'd always work together building things.

"Orv," Will said, "I've got an idea. This sled can do everything but steer. Maybe we can make a rudder for it. Then we can make it go to the right or to the left."

"We'll get Mother to draw one," Orv said.

"We'll draw one, you and I," Wilbur said. "We can't run to Mother every time we want to make something."

By now little Kate had come running down the hill.

"You promised," she panted. "You said you'd take me for a ride."

"Come on, Kate." Will laughed. "The three of us will coast down once. And then you can try it, Ed."

They trudged up the hill, pulling the sled. Two words kept singing in Wilbur's ears. "We flew . . . we flew . . . we flew. . . ."

3

Building a Wagon

The Reverend Milton Wright came home a few days later. Before he had his coat off he had to look at the new sled. He had to hear the story of how it had been made and how it was the fastest sled on the Big Hill.

"I let the boys use your tools," Susan Wright said.

There was a moment of silence. Reverend Wright liked to make things. He'd even made a typewriter once. He was very proud of his shining chisels, and sharp saws, and of his clean workbench out in the barn.

"You let the boys use my tools?" He was amazed.

"Yes, Father," Susan Wright said, while Will and Orv stood there feeling very nervous.

Without another word he turned and left the room. They heard him walking across the yard to the barn. It was ten minutes before he returned. He looked at the solemn faces of his two sons.

"You didn't hurt them any," he said with a twinkle in his eye. "As a matter of fact, someone sharpened some of my old chisels."

"When we were finished we sharpened all the tools," Will said eagerly.

"I felt they were old enough to take care of the tools," Mrs. Wright said.

"I guess you were right, Mother." Reverend Wright smiled.

"We want to use them again," Orv blurted out. "We want to make our sled steer."

"We want to build a rudder," Wilbur explained.

"Whoever heard of a rudder on a sled?" their father wanted to know.

"Father, we saw a picture of a boat in one of our schoolbooks," Wilbur said. "It had a rudder at the back. Maybe we can make a rudder that will steer our sled."

"Well, I don't know," his father said doubtfully.

"But look, Father." Wilbur ran to his father's desk and picked up a large piece of paper from it. "See? We drew a lot of pictures of a rudder and we think this one is the best."

"Let me see it." Reverend Wright looked at the neat drawing of a rudder. The measurements were all there in tiny penciled figures. It was to be a wooden rudder with a tiller. The rudder was attached to the back of the sled by two iron rings. Reverend Wright looked at his wife quickly.

"Bless my soul," he muttered. "They have your gift for drawing."

"They did this by themselves," she said proudly. "I didn't help them."

"It looks all right to me," Reverend Wright said.

"If it's right on paper, it'll be right when you make it," Wilbur said stoutly. "And we made a lot of drawings before we settled on this one."

"Where will you get the two iron rings?" their father asked.

"At the junk yard," Wilbur said. "Mr. Carmody gave them to us. And Father, when winter is over we're going to work for him. We're going to build a wagon and collect junk from the farmers and bring it to him."

"Well, one thing at a time. First see how your rudder works out," their father said.

"But Father . . ." Wilbur hesitated.

"I know. The tools," his father supplied, laughing. "Go on, boys, use the tools, but don't get hurt."

Soon the rudder wasn't just a drawing. It came into being out in the barn, and when the boys attached it to the back of the sled it just fitted. Once again the boys learned the truth of what their mother had said. They had been right to take so much time on their drawing.

That afternoon they tried the sled on the Big Hill. The other boys looked with curiosity at the odd thing attached to the back of the Wright boys' sled, but they didn't laugh. They would never laugh at the Wright brothers again. The sled, with Will holding the tiller, started to speed down the hill. Will turned the rudder and the sled swerved to the left; he turned it again and the sled swerved to the right. They could steer their sled, just as you could steer a boat.

That night a thaw set in. Then it rained for a whole week, a soft warm rain that washed away the snow and drowned the winter. Will and Orv trudged home from school every day over the muddy roads. They were no sooner home than they hurried to get their homework out of the way. They didn't like homework any more than anyone else did, but they knew it had to be done so they did it fast.

History, geography, spelling—these came slowly to the boys. But arithmetic was easy for them, and as they quickly finished the problems their teacher had given them, their mother smiled happily. Like their father, they enjoyed making things and they were happiest when they had tools in their hands. But their father was a great scholar who spoke and wrote beautiful English. He hadn't passed this on to his sons. And it was hard for him to add up a column of figures. The boys could do that easily. In this way they were like their mother.

Each day, after they had spent a half-hour or so on their homework, Orv would look up. "You finished, Will?" he would ask. Orv was always finished first. His grades were never as high as Will's, but he was very quick. Will took a little more time to think things out, but he nearly always gave the right answer.

Homework done, the boys would run to the barn to get through their chores. The wood box in the kitchen seemed to empty itself every few minutes. Their father had told them sternly, "Keep the wood box filled," and this was a job they never neglected. Will would saw the wood and then split the logs with an ax. He had a keen eye and he never missed. The sawed log would split in two as the sharp blade of the ax hit it. After that, Orv would gather up the split wood and run with it to the kitchen.

"That's enough, Will," he'd cry when the box beside the kitchen stove was full. Then Will would clean the ax and hang it in its place over the workbench.

Then both boys would run into the kitchen. "Wash your hands," their mother would call, and they'd hurry through that too. Finally they'd get paper, pencils, and ruler and sit down at the kitchen table. There was no hurrying them now. They were building a wagon, and a great deal depended upon this wagon.

Will and Orv had made a bargain with Mr.

Carmody, the junkman. He had told them that a lot of farmers in the outlying sections had junk to sell. Mr. Carmody didn't have a horse and buggy. And he didn't have time to go and see the farmers; he had to stay in his junk yard sorting out the metal and wooden articles that people sold him.

But if Wilbur and Orville had a wagon, they could go and pick up the things that the farmers couldn't use. The junkman would pay the boys for delivering the broken axes, the worn-out nuts and bolts, the broken chains, and wrecked bicycles that the farmers hadn't time to repair themselves. That was why the wagon was important to Will and Orv. Once they had a wagon they could go into business.

They had studied the wagons owned by their father's friends. *Their* wagon would have to be very light because they would have to pull it. It would have to be strong enough to carry iron and heavy metal of all kinds. The grocer in Dayton had a nice wagon, and they thought of copying it until they realized that the wheels were covered with strips of metal. These were "bought wheels," and the two boys didn't have any money to buy anything.

"We'll just have to make wooden wheels," Wilbur said, a bit discouraged.

Orv shook his head. "Ed Sines has a wagon with wooden wheels. Yesterday he lent it to me and I gave Kate a ride. I could hardly pull it at all. Wooden wheels are no good."

"Some of the farmers have ox carts that have wooden wheels," Wilbur said.

"But they have oxen to pull them," Orv reminded him. And then he had an idea. "You know what, Will?"

"What?" Wilbur had learned something during the past few weeks. He had learned to listen when Orv had a new idea. It was true that Orv was only eight, and Wilbur was twelve, but sometimes he startled Will.

"I've got it!" Orv cried. "Yesterday two old tricycles came into the junk yard. Mr. Carmody said they weren't much good. But I noticed that the wheels were okay. A lot of spokes were missing and some were broken, but maybe we could fix them with wire."

"Let's go see Mr. Carmody," Will said.

4

Their First Pocket Money

It was as Orv had said. The two tricycles were very old, but the wheels might be fixed. A lot of work had to be done, and it wouldn't be worth Mr. Carmody's time to fix them. Will and Orv told him they needed the wheels for their wagon, and Mr. Carmody smiled and said, "Suppose you fix the wheels. How are you going to attach them to your wagon?"

"We'll have to draw pictures of that first," Will said.

"Draw pictures?" Mr. Carmody was a little puzzled.

Then Wilbur explained. He told of how his mother always drew a pattern before she made herself a dress, and if she drew the pattern right the dress was right. He told about how he and Orv had made their sled. Mr. Carmody listened thoughtfully. And Orv told about how hard it was to pull Ed Sines's wagon with the wooden wheels.

"You're right, boys," he said. "You know, someone didn't just go out and build the first bicycle. Bicycles used to have heavy wooden wheels and thick iron tires. They used to weigh about a hundred pounds. They called 'em 'boneshakers,' and they sure did rattle your bones. You still see a lot of them around."

"Then what happened?" Orv asked.

"Well, some smart Frenchman started studying the bicycle," Mr. Carmody said. "He figured if you could make a lightweight bicycle, it would be easier to work it. You wouldn't get tired so fast. So he sat down and drew a bicycle that would be lighter than the old bonebreaker. He drew a light metal wheel with solid rubber tires cemented to the rims, and wooden spokes. He had someone make it up for him and it weighed half what the old-type bicycle weighed—and it went a lot faster."

"But now bicycles have wire spokes," Will said.

Mr. Carmody nodded. "Some other fellow—an American this time—set down and drew a wheel with wire spokes. That made it lighter and stronger. When he finished his drawing he said, 'That will make the bicycle better and stronger. That bicycle will carry ten times its own weight.' And he had some mechanic make one, and by golly the man was right!"

"His drawing was right, so the bicycle was right," Will said.

Mr. Carmody nodded. "Now, you've seen me on my bicycle. I weigh exactly two hundred pounds and my bicycle weighs just twenty pounds. You see, it carries ten times its weight. You make your wagon right and it'll carry ten times its weight. Now take those two old tricycles home with you and see if you can fix up those wheels. You'd better let me give you some heavy wire and take some axle grease with you, too. Those old wheels will stand a lot of grease."

Orv and Will hurried home, lugging the old tricycles (they had one big wheel in front and two smaller ones in back). They put the tricycles in the barn and ran to the house. As they sat at the kitchen table, full of ideas now, Ed Sines called in through the open window, "Come on, we're goin' fishin'."

"We got things to do," Will said, winking at Orv.

Neither Ed nor Chauncey Smith nor the other boys could understand why Will spent so much time with Orv. Why, Orv was four years younger, yet Will treated him as if he were Will's own age. So Ed and Chauncey went fishing and the Wright brothers leaned over their drawing.

Their mother came in and sat with them, but she was smart. She didn't offer advice. Not unless it was asked of her. And finally they did ask her what she thought of their plan to attach the wheels to their wagon. They had found two axles that fitted tightly into the hubs of the wheels.

Mrs. Wright shook her head. "Too much friction," she said.

"Friction?" Orv looked puzzled. He had never heard that word.

"You rub two sticks together—that's friction," she explained. "Rub them long enough and what happens?"

"They wear out," Orv said promptly.

"Well, the way you have these wheels fixed," she explained, "the hub of the wheel will keep rubbing against the axle. And before you know it the wheel will be worn out. There's too much friction. You can't get rid of all the friction, but you can lessen it. Maybe it'll work if you polish the end of the axle and polish the inside of the hub and then load it with axle grease."

Within a week they had their wagon finished.

It was spring now, and farmers were clearing out woodsheds and barns. Their wives, too, were having their annual spring cleaning, and that meant throwing junk out of closets, cellars, and attics.

Every day after school Will and Orv hurried home, got their wagon, and hauled it down the road out into the open country. Just before it was dark they'd come back with all kinds of odd-looking things in their wagon.

When summer vacation came they went right out after breakfast and were away all day. Mr. Carmody paid them well for the junk they collected, and now for the first time in their lives they had pocket money. Orv and

Will divided all the money they made. But what would they do with it? Once in a while on a Saturday they'd go to the candy store. There they'd buy a few all-day suckers or lemon drops or licorice sticks; but they worked too hard for their money to throw it all away on candy. They decided to buy a kite. They'd never had a "bought" kite.

At the general store in Dayton they looked the kites over. The box kites cost too much. The ordinary kites cost forty cents, and after long deliberation they picked one out.

That afternoon they went to the Big Hill with the boys. Their kite was all right—it was as good as Ed Sines's, but it wasn't any better. And, like all kites, it had a habit of suddenly diving, usually into a tree.

"I bet we could make a kite as good as this one, maybe better," Orv said. Wilbur looked thoughtful. They'd made a sled and a wagon, why not a kite? Why not a lot of kites? Maybe they could sell them to the boys.

"All right, Orv," Will said. "We'll make a good big kite for ourselves and then we'll make some to sell."

The wind was very strong that afternoon. As Orv held the kite string, a sudden gust of wind almost pulled it out of his hand.

"You know, Will," Orv said, chuckling, "maybe we could make a kite big enough to lift us right up into the air."

"Maybe we could," Wilbur answered, laughing; and then he stopped laughing. "By golly, someday we'll do that."

"Imagine being way up in the air hanging to a kite," Orv said.

"Like a bird," Will went on.

"But birds have wings," Orv said.

"We'll make our own wings," Wilbur said. "Kites will be our wings. Someday, Orv . . . someday . . ."

5
Making Kites

That was a busy year for the Wright brothers. They made their first kite. First they made a drawing of the skeleton of the kite. It had to be light, but it had to be strong, too. Getting light wood was not hard. They asked the grocer for some old wooden egg crates. He was only too glad to get rid of the boxes so easily.

Now that Will and Orv had their drawing and the right kind of wood, they had still another problem. They had noticed that the wood crosspieces of most kites were glued together. Sometimes if a kite hit a tree the crosspieces would become unstuck. To hold the pieces of wood together, they decided to use both glue and wire. Mr. Carmody, always helpful, gave them some old piano wire; it was light but it was strong.

Then the boys had another idea. They decided to make their kite bigger than the store kites the boys had been using. But what kind of wood could they use? The wood from the egg crates was all right for small kites, but it wasn't strong enough for anything larger, and the wood in the barn was too heavy.

Once again it was their mother who solved their problem. An old German cabinetmaker named Mr. Schwartz had opened a shop in Dayton. Mrs. Wright had asked him to fix an old chest of drawers she had been keeping in the attic for a long while. He fixed it beautifully. Mrs. Wright told her friends about this good carpenter and cabinetmaker, and some of them went to him. Mr. Schwartz was very grateful to Mrs. Wright for bringing him so many customers.

She took fourteen-year-old Will and ten-year-old Orv to the shop owned by Mr. Schwartz. He listened gravely while they explained what they wanted to do.

"I never made a kite," he said, "but I guess

you need a light wood that won't crack. I could give you some bamboo, but I think that would bend too easily. Suppose you try spruce for a starter."

He gave them enough wood to build a couple of kites. They hurried home and went to work. It didn't take long to make their skeleton, and then they covered it with tissue paper.

They wanted to try out the new kite when nobody was around, so they went to the Big Hill at six o'clock the next morning. There was a nice wind blowing, and the kite sailed right up into the air. It sailed way up, then climbed higher. Suddenly the wind seemed to die and the kite dove down straight into a tree.

Will climbed the tree and came down with the wreckage of the kite. The tissue paper which had covered it was in strips. The spruce skeleton was so smashed that it could never be fixed.

"I'm glad Ed and the boys weren't here," Orv said gloomily. "They'd laugh at us."

"We did something wrong," Will said, and then he added hopelessly, "but I don't know what."

"The drawing must have been wrong," Orv told him. "Otherwise the kite would have been all right."

Will nodded. "Well, Orv, after school today we'll make another drawing."

That afternoon they studied the old drawing. It certainly looked all right.

"What makes a kite dive, anyway?" Orv asked.

"I'm not sure," Will said, trying to think it out in his own mind. "Now the wind doesn't blow hard all the time. When it was blowing hard the kite stayed up there, didn't it?"

"That's right," Orv said.

"Then the wind died down and the kite just dove," Will said. "Maybe it dove because it wasn't getting enough wind. Sure, the wind had died down some, but it didn't die completely."

"Even a bird can soar along when there is hardly any wind," Orv said.

"I guess the wings of a bird are made so they can catch even a little bit of wind," Will told him. Then he raised his head sharply. "Orv, maybe that's the trouble. Our kite wasn't getting enough wind. Why?"

"Maybe . . . maybe the bellyband was too tight," Orv said. The kites flown by boys then had a bellyband and a tail made of knotted cloth.

"Maybe," Will said, excited now, "when the bellyband is too tight the kite can't billow out like a sail and catch the wind. That doesn't matter when there's a lot of wind, but when the wind dies down there's nothing to keep the kite up there."

"Let's try a longer bellyband," Orv said, so they leaned over the kitchen table and drew a longer bellyband.

"Will," Orv asked, "what does the tail of a kite do?"

"I think it's supposed to balance the kite," Will said doubtfully. He wasn't quite sure.

"I noticed that when there's hardly any wind, sometimes a kite won't go up at all. I guess that's because its tail is too heavy."

"That's right." Will nodded. "I have an idea that you need a long tail when there's a lot of wind and hardly any tail at all when there isn't much wind. When we make our kite we'll try it out with a long tail and then with a short tail."

Luckily they had enough spruce left over to make the second kite. They made the belly-band longer.

At six the next morning they were out on the Big Hill. Again the wind was strong, but it wasn't a steady wind. It blew in gusts. They sent the new kite up and it climbed all right, but once it was up there it seemed unsteady; it swerved from side to side.

"I don't think the tail is long enough to balance it," Orv said. They brought the kite down and added a foot of knotted cloth to the tail. This time the kite flew as though it had wings. It climbed steadily and stayed up in the air without a sign of swerving or diving.

"Look at it," Orv said. "The kite billows out like a sail."

"That's because the bellyband is long enough. Even when the wind dies down the tissue paper catches it all and the kite stays up there. I bet we could fly this kite a mile high," Will said.

"We'll try it out this afternoon," Orv said.

That afternoon all the boys were at the Big Hill.

The new kite flew higher than any other kite. It didn't dive; it just sailed lazily up into the sky. The boys all wanted to try it, so Will gave each one a chance.

"You wouldn't want to trade for it?" Al Johnston asked.

Will looked at Orv. They both thought awhile. They couldn't think of anything Al had they wanted.

"No," Wilbur said. "But we'll sell it."

"How much?" Al asked.

"Twenty cents," Wilbur said, not very hopefully.

Al Johnston hesitated. He got fifty cents a week for delivering groceries after school. But twenty cents was a lot to pay for a homemade kite.

"The one you got cost you forty cents," Wilbur reminded him, "and it's no good."

Al nodded. That was true enough.

"All right, I'll buy it," he said. "But I don't get paid until Saturday."

"We'll wait," Will said. "Here's your kite, Al."

They made plenty of kites after that. They finally made some box kites with cloth instead of tissue paper. They flew higher than the ordinary kites, but they were hard to make.

Orv had an idea one day. "Maybe we can

fly two at once," he said to Will. "Let one way out and then tie another kite to the string. Let's see what happens."

"All right," Will said, a little doubtfully.

It worked beautifully. They let out half their string and then attached the second kite. Away it went. Orv was holding it.

"Feel the pull on it, Will," he said excitedly. "I can hardly hold it."

Will grabbed the string. What Orv had said was true. Orv let out more string. Now the second kite was soaring into the sky.

"It almost lifts me off the ground, Will," Orv laughed. "Someday we'll make a kite that'll carry us up. . . ."

Then it happened. The strain of two kites pulling was too much for the old string they'd been using. Somewhere overhead the string snapped and there, soaring away as free as birds, were the two box kites. Will and Orv never saw either of them again.

6

Wilbur's Illness

Neither Wilbur nor Orville spent all of their time making things. Wilbur was at high school now, and the school had just added a new gymnasium. The gym had a horizontal bar and Will spent most of his time working on this. Every day he chinned himself, and soon he had no trouble pulling himself up to the bar fifty times without stopping. His arms and hands were strong.

After six months he was able to do the hardest trick of all on the horizontal bar—the giant swing. He hung on the bar, swung back and forth until he felt he was ready, and then swung all the way around the bar. The gymnasium teacher tried to get him interested in the parallel bars and in calisthenics, but all he cared about was that giant swing.

"It's like flying," he told Orv.

Wilbur grew stronger every day. There were no buses in those days (a man named Henry Ford was just beginning to make his "horseless carriage"), so both Wilbur and Orv had to walk to school. It was two miles each way, and this constant walking made their legs strong.

Wilbur, even as a freshman at high school, was a star on the football team. In the winter he played hockey. The high-school team had games on a frozen pond near the school.

One day they played against a team made up of the sons of officers who were stationed at a nearby army post. It was a fierce, hard game and the score was 1 to 1. Wilbur had scored the goal for his team.

One of the army boys snared the puck with his stick. Wilbur skated right into him, knocking the puck away. Then there was a wild scramble for it. One of the army boys took a wild swing at the puck. He missed the puck but he didn't miss Wilbur. His stick caught Wilbur right on the mouth. Wilbur stood there a little dazed—then he spit five teeth out. The game stopped. Luckily there was an army doctor watching the game. He rushed over to Wilbur.

"That must hurt a lot, son," he said.

"Naw—it doesn't hurt," Wilbur said, and then he toppled over in a faint.

They took him home and put him to bed. Penicillin and sulfanilamide (used to treat bacteria and infections) weren't known in those days. Doctors just poured iodine on a cut and hoped it would heal. The treatment didn't work with Wilbur. His nasty cuts became infected; three more teeth had to be taken out. For weeks Wilbur could take only liquid food through a tube. Then the doctors let him have eggs and toast. For some strange reason the diet didn't agree with him. It gave him stomach trouble and weakened his heart. It almost looked as though he'd be an invalid the rest of his life.

His mother and father and Orv took turns sitting with him. His father didn't take any trips now. He'd sit at Will's bedside talking, and Will would listen quietly. For the first time he really learned to know his father well. Will asked him how he had happened to become a minister, and his father explained that some people just had the call to be ministers—others didn't.

Wilbur would lie there thinking over what his father had said about God and about religion. He'd think up new questions to ask his father. He and Orv never took things for granted. They always asked why. Finally Will told his father that when he got better he was going to help him all he could. Maybe he too would become a minister.

His wise father shook his head and smiled. "Each one of us is given a task to do by God," he said. "I don't think he wants either you or Orville to be ministers. I don't know what plans he has for you. I think they are big plans."

When Wilbur was well enough to sit up in bed, his father bought him a wood-carving and drawing set. Now Wilbur was happy. He had sharp, delicate chisels of his own and lovely soft wood that could be carved into all sorts of shapes. A book came with the wood-carving set. It explained about maple and spruce and ash and other kinds of wood. Some were lighter than others. Some would bend without breaking. Some light wood was even stronger than heavy wood. Wilbur might never have learned all this if he hadn't been hurt in the hockey game.

One day Orv came in.

"You know what, Will?"

"What, Orv?"

"Let's make Mother a chair," Orv said excitedly. "You draw one and I'll do the heavy work out in the barn. We'll keep it secret."

It was nearly always like that. Orv had the first quick idea. Will would think it over, weigh it, and then the two of them would talk it over.

Now they drew the kind of chair they knew their mother would like. Real drawing paper, the right kind of pencils, a ruler, and even a compass to draw circles had come with the drawing set, and Will had been practicing. The drawing he made was a professional piece of work.

Orv sneaked out to the barn to do the rest. Will sat in bed, directing the work. A chair isn't easy to build. First four round holes must be made in the seat part. Into these holes the four legs are fitted. Luckily the boys' father had a brace and a whole lot of bits. One was a ¾-inch bit. And Orv found a couple of old broomsticks that were just three-quarters of an inch thick. These made legs that fitted perfectly.

Orv ran down to Mr. Schwartz's shop to "borrow" some glue, and when the glue had dried the boys had a good sturdy chair. They made a back for it and then Orv painted it. The next morning when their mother walked into the kitchen to get breakfast ready, there was the new chair. It was the first present her sons had ever made her. Oh, they always bought her Christmas and birthday presents, but this was different. They'd made this chair with their own hands and she was proud of it.

The wood-carving set and his work with Orv weren't enough to keep Wilbur busy, even though he was sick. He also read a lot lying in bed. He'd never read much before, except the books that were part of his schoolwork. Now he discovered reading. He found out how exciting books could be. His favorite was *Robinson Crusoe* because Robinson Crusoe landed on that island without anything at all. He had to make everything. He made a raft, then a hut, and soon he made himself tools and even clothes. If he hadn't been good at making things, he would have died.

Will would lie back and make believe that he and Orv were wrecked on a desert island. They'd get along all right because they could make things, too. He dreamed that he and Orv would be famous someday, but of course he never really believed that his dreams would ever come true. He didn't know then that dreams *can* come true. Sometimes they need a little help, that's all.

Orv scarcely ever read. He didn't want to read about other people's ideas. He had ideas of his own. That's all he cared about. And he thought that if you kept reading books you had no time to make things. For instance, he and Ed Sines had gone into partnership. They had chipped in and bought a little printing press. They were both in the graduating class at grammar school now, and they decided to get out a school paper called the *Midget*. They named it after their printing press, which was only about as big as a cigar box.

But the press worked. They wrote about their schoolmates and set the type and out it came. But paper and ink cost money. They decided to ask the grocer, the butcher, Mr. Carmody at the junk yard, and Mr. Schwartz to advertise in their paper. An advertisement cost fifteen cents. Everyone they asked bought ads in the *Midget*. Of course the small printing press could only print a little paper.

"Wait till Will gets better," Orv said to Ed Sines. "We can make a printing press ourselves. A big one."

"You're crazy," Ed said.

"We made a sled; we made a kite; we made a chair," Orv said. "We can make anything. You wait and see."

Finally Wilbur was well enough to get up. His mother and father decided not to send him back to school. He was too weak to walk two miles each way every day.

At that time Reverend Wright was editor of a church paper named the *Christian Conservator*. He decided to give Wilbur a job. His job was to fold the papers as they came off the press and place them in envelopes. Because everyone liked the minister so much, a great many people wanted to read his weekly paper, and Wilbur found it took a long time to fold all those papers. Finally Orv came in to help him, but he found it dull work.

"We ought to build a folding machine," Orv said one day.

"I never heard of a folding machine," Will said.

"Me neither," Orv told him. "But I bet we could figure out something. . . ."

"Mr. Schwartz has a lathe in his shop," Will said thoughtfully. "It works by a foot treadle. Maybe we . . ."

"There's a lot of old junk in the yard behind this print shop," Orv said. "I noticed some rollers. Now if we . . ."

That night they leaned over the kitchen table. They were used to working together now. Orv kept throwing out quick ideas and Will would try to find something wrong with them. If he couldn't, they'd try out the ideas. Gradually a weird-looking machine began to take shape on the drawing board. This was the hardest job they'd tried yet, because they were working with metal. But three weeks later there it stood, made completely of parts they had found.

No one but the two boys could work it. While Will kept pumping with his foot, Orv kept feeding papers to the machine. Darned if the papers didn't come out neatly folded and just the right size!

Their father stared in amazement. It usually took Wilbur and Orville two days to fold the papers. This funny-looking machine had done the work in two hours!

Reverend Wright looked at his two sons solemnly. "When you were sick, Will," he said, "I told you I thought God had big plans for you and Orv. Now I know what he wants you to be. He wants you to be inventors. You'll spend the rest of your life making new things that will help mankind."

"We can make anything," Orv said confidently. "Even a printing press."

"We can't make everything," Will said, "but we can try to make things that no one has ever made before."

"We'll make a kite that will carry us way up into the air," Orv said.

"You are boys—not birds," their father said, smiling.

"Maybe Orv is right, Father," Wilbur said. "Maybe we will fly someday. Maybe we will."

7
The Helicopter

When Reverend Wright returned from a trip he nearly always brought presents. Wilbur's gift was usually a book. Kate would receive a new doll to add to her collection. Orville had very special tastes. Above all, he had always liked toy soldiers. He had a whole set of Revolutionary War soldiers and of Civil War soldiers, too. He would place his armies on the floor and "fight" them. But now he was growing a bit too old to play with soldiers. Reverend Wright always had trouble picking out a present that Orville would like.

He returned from one trip with a new kind of toy. Orville had outgrown ordinary toys, but this one was different. It was called a helicopter. It was an unusual object made of bamboo covered with tissue paper. It had two odd-looking things attached to it that looked exactly like the propellers that drove boats. These propellers could be wound up; a rubber band was attached to each.

"We'd better try it outside," their father said, catching Mother Wright's eye.

The two boys were more puzzled than excited. They just didn't know what to make of this new toy. They followed their father outside. He wound up the two propellers and then released the toy. It darted right up into the air about fifteen feet, and then dropped to the ground.

"It's like a flying bat," Orville cried out.

"It's a kite without a tail," Will said, excited now.

"I don't know what it is," their father said. "I never saw anything like it. They call it a helicopter."

"Hell-uh-cop-ter," Orville repeated.

"It's from the Greek," their father said. "*Helico* means something of spiral formation; *pteron* is 'wing.' It means a wing that moves in a spiral."

By now Will had rewound the little toy. Once again it left his hand the way a bird would leave it, except that it flew straight up. Orville and Wilbur had inquiring minds. Other boys might look at such a toy and say, "How fast does it go? How high does it go?" Orv and Wilbur asked themselves just one question: "What makes it go?" They noticed that the two little propeller fans went around in different directions. That was strange in itself.

"When this thing goes straight up it must push a hole in the air," Wilbur said.

Orv nodded. "Or it just pushes the air aside, the way a propeller on a boat pushes the water away."

They took their toy apart, rebuilt it, and flew it again and again. It puzzled and annoyed them a little bit because they didn't understand why the toy went straight up. Why didn't it go like a bird or like a kite? Of course they were asking themselves questions to which great scientists of that time were trying to find the answers, and it is easy to understand why the two boys were puzzled. Finally, one day, the little toy, rising quickly, smashed into the branch of a big tree that stood in front of the house, and they were never able to patch it up again. But they didn't forget the "helicopter."

At best, though, it had only been a toy. A toy made by somebody else. Neither Wilbur nor Orville cared much about things other people made. They only wanted things they had made themselves. Their father encouraged them; he felt that there was something special about these two sons of his. So did Mrs. Wright. When other mothers asked her, "What are the boys doing? We never see them around with our sons," she'd smile a sort of secret smile and say, "Oh, they're puttering around in the barn."

They were indeed puttering around in the barn. Orv had told Ed Sines that he and Wilbur would make a real printing press. A big printing press works just about the same as a little printing press. Wilbur and Orv had studied the way the little press worked, and now in the barn they were making one twenty times as big.

The old junk yard was a real gold mine for them. It was filled with all sorts of stuff that no one wanted, and Mr. Carmody didn't mind letting Wilbur and Orv cart some of it home with them. For instance, there was an old iron roller lying there, part of some machine a farmer had once used. The boys took it home, scraped the rust off it, and polished it, and that became part of their printing press. They went all over the countryside looking for a big flat stone on which to put the type, and finally they found one.

The part of the press they couldn't make was the type. That had to be bought, and it cost about fifteen dollars. Between them they had saved about ten dollars, but their mother lent them the extra five.

Making a press was new to Orv and Will, but the idea was an old one. The Chinese invented printing a thousand years ago. It wasn't until 1454 that printing became popular in Europe. Then a German named Johann Gutenberg printed the Bible on his printing press, and now we usually say that the printing press was invented by Johann Gutenberg. He didn't really invent it; he *improved* it, and was the first man ever to print a book from movable type.

The big, funny-looking printing press that Wilbur and Orv made probably looked something like Gutenberg's printing press. Anyhow, the principle was the same. The type was set up and put on a flat stone or "bed." (That's what the printers call it.) The type was inked, a sheet of paper was put over it, and then the roller was run over it. The inked type came off on the paper. That was the principle. Of course it took a long time to print a lot of copies of anything because the roller had to be operated by hand. It was like rolling a tennis court.

But that wasn't good enough for Wilbur and Orv. They fixed up a foot treadle. Their mother had a sewing machine then, and they had noticed how she worked it. Her right foot pumped up and down on the foot treadle and that made the needle go up and down at a very fast rate.

So they made a foot treadle for their printing press. They attached pulleys to the roller and now the heavy roller moved back and forth, back and forth, as long as you pumped the foot treadle. Wilbur would work it and Orv would "feed" paper to the flat bed of the printing press. He'd pull out the printed sheet and then, before the roller had time to come back, he'd slip another sheet onto the type. Now and then the boys had to stop to ink the type.

Finally the printing press was finished. It actually worked. But what good was a printing press if you had nothing to print?

8

The West Side *Tatler*

"We ought to get out a weekly newspaper, Will," Orville said.

"But we have no money," Wilbur answered gloomily. His father had been named Bishop of the Pacific Coast, which meant he had to give up his church paper and travel again. That was a blow to Will and Orv, because their father had been paying each of them two dollars a week for folding the papers.

"If we had a newspaper we could run advertisements, the way Ed and I did with our school paper," Orv said. "And we'd make money."

"But first we need money to buy ink and

paper and we need some new type, too," Wilbur said.

"We can't ask Mother again," Orv said. "We still owe her five dollars."

"I can get a job delivering groceries," Will said. "And you and Ed Sines can go out collecting junk."

"If we work all summer, we ought to have at least thirty dollars saved," Orv said. "But Will, the doctor said you shouldn't do any hard work."

"Delivering groceries isn't hard work," Wilbur said.

"The doctor said you shouldn't lift heavy things," Orv insisted. "I tell you what, Will. You get the job and I'll work with you. We'll get out the old wagon and grease it up. We can deliver the groceries in that."

And that's what they did. No two brothers were ever closer. They liked Ed Sines and the other boys, but best of all they liked to be by themselves. They'd talk about things that the other fellows didn't understand. As they pulled the wagon along they talked about kites they had made, about that expression "wind resistance" their mother had taught them, about the funny flying toy, the helicopter, about the new bicycles that were coming out.

"We might make ourselves a couple of bicycles someday," Orv said solemnly. Bicycles were expensive (even second-hand ones), and their father had never been able to buy one for them.

"Wait till we get our newspaper going," Will said. "You know, Orv, we'll need a bicycle then to deliver the paper. We'd better start looking for spare parts of old bicycles. Maybe we can get enough of them to make one whole bicycle."

Both of them kept their eyes open. They found an old frame of a bicycle; they found a front wheel that could be fixed; they found handlebars that could be straightened out. Soon all these were piled in their barn. Someday they'd have enough parts to make a bike.

Meanwhile they hauled butter and eggs and bread and flour and vegetables to the people in town. Everybody by now knew the "Bishop's sons." They were polite, rather serious-looking young men. They didn't laugh much or say much unless they were alone with each other.

"When we start our newspaper," Wilbur said, "we'll have to print stories about the people in town, so let's keep our eyes open and remember things."

When they delivered groceries to Farmer Brown, they might hear that the farmer had a chicken that had laid a record number of eggs, or that he had bought a new bull. If the mayor's daughter had whooping cough they found out about it, and if a new family came to town they learned about that, too. Each week when they were paid, they'd take their money and put it in a drawer of their father's desk. There were not many picnics that summer with their mother and sister Kate, and Wilbur and Orv didn't have much fun, but they didn't mind. The only thing that mattered was to make enough money to start their weekly newspaper. And when summer ended they did have enough.

Then they could get out their paper. They wrote down all the stories they had heard and set them in type. Kate helped them and they took in Ed Sines as a partner. They called their paper West Side *Tatler*, and the day the first issue came off the press was a proud day for them all.

Twenty-one-year-old Wilbur was editor, and seventeen-year-old Orville was business manager. Orv hurried to every merchant in town with the newspaper, and most of them promised to advertise regularly.

A hundred copies of the paper were printed each week, and Ed Sines and a couple of boys delivered them. Now Wilbur and Orv were happy again. They were making something. They were making a paper—and they were always tinkering with the printing press, trying to improve it.

They had to work hard because the type had to be set by hand. Orv had very sure, quick fingers, and he could set type much faster than Wilbur or Kate. Orville was always the quick one.

Everybody liked the paper. And they kept on buying it. A year after the first issue, the circulation had risen to three hundred copies a week, and the Wright brothers' profits were usually about fifteen dollars each week. Will and Orv saved every cent of it.

In their spare time they "made" a bicycle. They didn't really make it; they assembled it out of old parts and bought a few new parts, and now they owned a bicycle. It wasn't new or shiny, and every now and then one of the old parts collapsed, but the two brothers could always fix the bike. They could fix anything.

Smart Orville, the business manager, had an idea one day.

"When the church prints a bulletin or a store wants to print a notice of a sale," he said, "they always let some big printing firm do the job for them. Why don't we do job printing?"

"It's an idea," Wilbur said. "Our press is busy only two days a week. You go around and see if you can get us some jobs to do."

After Orville found how much the regular printers charged, he told everyone that he and Wilbur would do the job for half that. Now they were really busy, because the merchants were naturally anxious to get their printing done as cheaply as possible. With the help of this added business, Will and Orv were making twenty-five, sometimes thirty dollars a week and saving a good deal of it. In a year's time they saved nearly a thousand dollars.

But they were gradually losing interest in their paper. Why? Well, all they had to do was to collect stories, set them in type, print the paper, and deliver it. It was too easy. It had been fun at first because it was hard work and the printing press kept breaking down and they'd have to fix it. They were really happy only when they were fixing things or making things.

When Ed Sines broke his bicycle it was fun to fix it. That was what they really liked to do. As usual, it was Orville who had the idea of using their money to open a bicycle shop.

"You see more and more bicycles on the road every day," he told Wilbur. "The roads are pretty bad, and people are always having spills. They break spokes and even wheels."

"That's an idea, Orv," Will said slowly. "Maybe we could sell our paper to Ed and rent a store."

"I already did," Orv said calmly. "I knew you'd like the idea."

Wilbur laughed. It was just like Orv to go right ahead with some new idea.

"We have plenty of tools," Orv said. "We'll move them to the store. We have a lot of old spare parts."

"You have it all figured out," Wilbur said.

"Sure I have," Orv said happily. "After a

while we might even make bicycles and sell them."

"What'll we call our store?" Will asked, knowing that Orv had already thought of that, too.

"The Wright Cycle Company," Orville said proudly.

9

The Wright Cycle Company

The first thing Wilbur and Orv did was to have some stationery printed with the name "Wright Cycle Co." in big letters. Under that it said:

WILBUR WRIGHT, *President*
ORVILLE WRIGHT, *Vice President*

Most people in Dayton owned the old-fashioned bicycles—whose front wheel was bigger than the back wheel. The bicycles didn't have brakes or coasters or even mud-guards, and they had solid rubber tires. But lately a new bike had come out. Both its wheels were the same size. Most important of all, it had the kind of tires that bicycles have now—the kind that are pumped up.

Will and Orv wrote to the firm in Springfield, Massachusetts, that was making the new bicycles and said they'd like to represent them. When the owner of the big factory in Massachusetts read the letter, he was very impressed. He probably thought it had come from two established businessmen. And he replied that the Wright Cycle Company could sell his company's spare parts.

About this time someone started a bicycle club in Dayton. Every Saturday and Sunday boys of all ages would go on long trips, and when they came home, as often as not something had gone wrong with the bikes that needed fixing.

Wilbur and Orv were right there with their tools and their spare parts. They bought a second-hand bike from their pal Ed Sines and fixed it up with the new spare parts. They even added two new wheels to it.

One day as they worked on their bike, Orv exclaimed, "I've got an idea!"

"You're always getting ideas," said Wilbur, laughing.

"I've been trying out this bike of ours,

Will," Orv said. "And you want to know something?"

"What?" Will asked.

"Well, for some reason it's faster than any of the other bikes around, even the new one Al Stewart has. Al is three years older than I am, but I can beat him in a race. You know why?"

Will shook his head.

"Because we took Ed's old bike apart and cleaned every bit of it," Orv said. "Then we added the new parts. Every bit of our bike is clean and shiny because we sandpapered it and polished it. Remember Mother telling us about friction a long time ago? Well, I figure if you keep every part of your bike clean, that means there is less friction and you can travel faster."

"You're leading up to something, Orv." Wilbur could always tell when Orv had an idea that might work.

"Well, it's this," Orv said. "I think I can beat anyone around here in a bike race. So let's have a race some Saturday afternoon and I'll enter it. If I win, the fellows will all want bikes like the one I'm riding."

"What of it?" Wilbur asked.

"Don't you see? We'll sell them bikes!" Orv said triumphantly. "A new bike costs a hundred dollars. Well, there aren't three fellows in town whose fathers can afford a hundred dollars for a bike. But we can buy up all the old, broken-down bikes in town. I bet we can get them for maybe five dollars each. We'll use their frames, add new tires and wheels (the kind with ball bearings), give them a good coat of paint, and make them shine. I bet we can get maybe thirty dollars each for them."

"Not a bad idea," Will said. "But first you have to win some races."

"I'm going to start training now," Orv said. "I'm going to ride five miles every morning, and when I'm ready I'll organize the race. We'll get people in town to offer prizes for the winners. *We'll* give the prize for first place—a brand new tool kit. A good kit with all the tools anyone would need to fix anything, and a pump, too."

"It'll cost about ten dollars," Wilbur said. "That's pretty steep."

"You forgot something, Will," Orv said slyly.

"What did I forget?" Will was puzzled.

"You forgot I'm going to win first prize," Orv said calmly.

Orv started training the next day. He'd get up at six in the morning, hop on the bike, and pedal out into the country. Pedaling five miles on rough roads isn't easy, but Orv stuck to it and gradually his legs became strong.

In those days you couldn't raise and lower the handlebars of a bike as you can do now. One day Wilbur noticed that Orv was bending over the bike, sawing off the handlebars.

"What are you doing?" he asked.

"I got an idea," Orv said calmly. "These handlebars are pretty high. Last week there was a picture in the paper of a horse race. The jockey on the horse that won was leaning right down on the horse's neck. Why? Because there wasn't so much wind resistance that way. Remember the first sled Mother helped us make? She said to make it low, close to the ground, so there wouldn't be so much wind resistance. It's the same with a bike. I'm going to lower these handlebars. Then when I ride I'll be leaning over and getting under the wind."

"Sounds like a good idea," Wilbur said.

Orv finished sawing off the handlebars; he

shortened the metal upright that held them and then he soldered the handlebars back to the upright. When he climbed on his bike he was bent way over. When he tried it out he was surprised to find that not only could he go faster, but also that he wasn't as tired when he finished. His back didn't ache as it did when he sat almost upright.

Orv got Ed Sines to announce in the paper that there would be a two-mile bike race the next Saturday at the Fair Grounds. Everyone who owned a bike could enter the race. The first prize would be the tool kit and pump. Orv spoke to the grocer for whom he and Wilbur had worked. It didn't take him long to persuade the grocer to donate a dozen jars of jelly and jam as second prize. The butcher gave a ham for third prize.

Not only the young fellows but also some of the older men who owned bicycles entered the race. The night before, Wilbur and Orv took their bike completely apart. They cleaned every bit of dirt out of the hub. They even shined the spokes. They oiled the bike and then put it together again.

"I'll finish this, Orv," Will said. "This is one night you're going to get a good sleep."

Then he added, "How are the tires?"

"They're all right," Orv said casually. "I've been using them a month and never had a puncture."

10

The Bicycle Race

There were twenty bikes lined up at the starting line the next afternoon. About half of the racers were older men, and Orv felt a little nervous as he looked at them. But this was a two-mile race, and it could be pretty tiring to anybody who hadn't trained. Orville's legs were like steel springs now. He knew he could pedal the two miles without becoming exhausted.

One man had a brand-new bicycle called the Columbia. This was made in Hartford, Connecticut, and Orv looked at it curiously. It was the very latest bicycle out, and Orv noticed that it had handlebars you could raise or lower. It was the first bicycle he'd ever seen with adjustable handlebars.

Jack Winters, who was about thirty, owned the new bicycle and he was certainly proud of it. But Orv knew that Jack Winters was head bookkeeper at the local mill company and that Jack worked very hard. He spent ten hours every day bent over his ledgers. His bike was certainly the best one Orv had ever seen, but he didn't think that Jack could be a very good bike rider. The poor man worked so hard, he never had time for exercise.

Orv noticed another thing. Jack hadn't lowered his handlebars. They were very high, and when Winters climbed on his bike he was sitting almost straight up. Orv was sure that Jack could go a lot faster if he would lower his handlebars, but he wasn't going to tell him.

"There's a real stiff wind blowing, Orv," Wilbur said in a low voice. "Let the others get out in front and fight that wind. You stay behind for the first mile. They'll get the full force of the wind; you won't. Fighting that wind will tire them out. Then when they're tired, move ahead."

Ed Sines was the starter. He lined them up and called, "Ready...get set...GO." They were off. Everyone tried to get out in front. Orv stayed behind, leaning way over his handlebars like a jockey over the neck of a horse. Jack Winters was a big man and Orv stuck close behind him. Winters was fighting the wind. Orv didn't even feel it, for Jack Winters was acting as a kind of windshield for him.

The race was held on a half-mile track that was used for trotting races in the summertime. At the finish of the first lap Orville was in tenth place. At the end of the second lap he was in fifth place. He wasn't exerting himself. He was just trying to stay within twenty yards of the leaders. And he wasn't a bit tired. At the end of the third lap Orv was in fourth place. He caught Wilbur's eye and gave him a reassuring wink. Wilbur yelled, "Now go on, step on it!"

Orv started after the leaders, who were only ten yards in front of him. He passed one...another...still another, and now only Jack Winters on his new Columbia was ahead of him. But Winters was tired and puffing badly. They came into the homestretch and now they were even. Orv hadn't even drawn a deep breath.

"Now I'll put on speed and go right past him," Orv said to himself. He leaned even lower over his handlebars and started to pedal furiously. He heard the cries from the crowd at the finish line. Gradually he drew away from Winters. He was five yards in front, with only a hundred yards to go. Orv was laughing to himself. This was going to be easy, he thought lightheartedly.

And then disaster struck. With a loud bang his front tire exploded. The wheel wobbled and then turned sharply to the right. Orv pitched right over the handlebars. He lay there unhurt but discouraged, sick at heart. Winters pedaled by him, called out a cheerful "Tough luck, Orv," and crossed the line an easy winner. Orv got to his feet and picked up his bike. At least he could finish second. But then he noticed that the front wheel was all out of shape. The spill had wrecked it.

Wilbur came running up. "You all right, Orv?" he panted.

"Sure," Orv said, his face gloomy and discouraged. "I had him beat, Will. It was just bad luck I got that puncture."

"No it wasn't," Wilbur said seriously. "It was our carelessness. Go up and congratulate Jack Winters, Orv."

Orv didn't know what Wilbur meant by the phrase "our carelessness." He only knew that he had lost and he had been so sure of winning. He stood silent while Ed Sines presented Winters with the brand-new tool kit and pump, and he winced when he thought of the ten dollars they had cost Wilbur and himself.

The other fellows teased Orv about his spill, but he was in no mood for teasing. Mr. Henry, who owned the mill company, was so happy because Jack Winters had won that he announced there would be another race the next Saturday and that he would put up an Ingersoll watch as first prize.

"Let's get this broken bike to the shop," Wilbur said, and he and Orv trudged sadly away. Wilbur didn't say much until they reached the shop. They carried the bike inside. Then Wilbur looked sternly at Orv.

"It was my fault as well as yours, Orv," he said solemnly. "When you said 'These tires are all right. I've been using them a month and never had a puncture,' I should have insisted that we put new tires on the wheels."

"But they looked all right," Orv said unhappily.

"Let this be a lesson to us, Orv," Wilbur said. "Sure, the tires looked all right, but we should have known that the average tire is only good for about ten hours of bicycling. Then it gets worn down a bit. If we had really examined that front tire, we would have found a couple of soft spots where it was worn almost through."

"New tires would have cost so much," Orv pointed out.

"I know," Wilbur told him. "But if we'd put new tires on the bike, you would have won, and maybe by now someone would be ordering a bike from us."

"I guess I was overconfident, Will," Orv said miserably.

"We both were," Wilbur said. "After this we'll never take things for granted. We'll examine every part of a machine before we use it, whether it's a printing press or a lathe or a bike or . . . or a kite."

"Well, let's get to work," Orv said. "Luckily we have two new tires in stock."

It didn't take them long to replace the front

wheel and to put brand-new tires on both wheels.

Wilbur noticed that business fell off during the week. People with bicycles to be fixed took them elsewhere.

Ed Sines told them why.

"People say, 'If the Wright brothers can't even keep their own bicycle in good repair, how can they expect to fix our bikes?' " he told Wilbur and Orv.

"Wait till next Saturday," Orv said grimly. He wasn't overconfident now—just determined.

When Orv appeared at the starting line the next Saturday he was greeted by loud laughter. Jack Winters was there again with his new bike, and Johnny Morrow had a new one, too; his father had bought him a Columbia during the week.

"We might have sold one of our bikes if I'd won last week," Orv said to Wilbur.

"Stop blaming yourself," Wilbur said sharply. "It was my fault as well as yours. You're going to win today because this bike is in perfect condition."

Mr. Henry was the starter this time. He called them all to the starting line. A big crowd was watching. Nearly everyone thought that Jack Winters would win easily.

And then they were off. There was no wind at all, and Orv decided to go right out in front and stay there. At the end of the first lap he was ten yards ahead of Jack Winters. At the end of the second lap he was twenty yards ahead of him. Then he really started to pedal. The crowd was silent now in amazement. Orv was leaning way over, pedaling furiously. At the end of the third lap he was a hundred yards in front of Jack Winters and he had lapped nearly all of the other contestants. He kept on pedaling, and he kept pulling away from Jack Winters and the field. He won by a quarter of a mile.

Wilbur slapped Orv on the shoulder and said, "Nice going, Orv," and from his face you'd never know that he was the proudest young man at the Fair Grounds. Mr. Henry made a little speech and then he presented Orv with the watch. It was the first watch Orv had ever owned.

"By the way, Orv," Mr. Henry said, "That's quite a bike you have there. I'd like to buy one like it for my boy. What make is it?"

Wilbur blinked. He wouldn't have known how to answer that question.

But Orville was never at a loss for an answer. "We make it ourselves, Mr. Henry," he said casually. "We call it . . . we call it . . ." he added with a flash of inspiration, "the Wright Flier."

11

In the Bicycle Business

That week the Wright brothers received three orders for bicycles. But they had only about eighty dollars now between them; everything else had gone into the shop. To assemble new bikes meant that they would have to buy up old ones and then buy wheels, tires, new seats, even new handlebars, and all these things would cost money. They felt pretty gloomy about it. Their sister Kate, who was always around the shop, heard them talking about it, but she didn't say anything. She just slipped out of the shop and went home.

That night after the supper dishes were washed and put away, the two brothers sat in the living room, not saying much. Their mother was sewing. She made all of Kate's clothes and she even made shirts for Wilbur and Orv.

"I'm very proud of you two," Mrs. Wright said now. "Mrs. Henry was saying today that you're making a bicycle for her son."

"Mr. Henry ordered a new bike from us," Wilbur admitted.

"I wish I could be a partner of yours," their mother said, never raising her eyes from her sewing. "You know, I've saved nearly three hundred dollars and it's just lying in the bank. Why don't you let me buy a third interest in the shop with that three hundred dollars?"

Orv leaped to his feet. "You mean it, Mother?" he asked excitedly.

"Of course," she said calmly. "Any mother would be glad to be a partner with her two sons. I know you don't need the money at the moment. . . ."

"Not much we don't!" Orv shouted. "With that sum we can buy enough spare parts to make a dozen bicycles."

"I spoke to Mr. Gentry at the bank this afternoon," Mrs. Wright said, "and told him you could draw on it."

"How did you know we needed money, Mother?" Wilbur asked suspiciously.

"Why . . . why, I just wanted to be your partner," Mrs. Wright said.

Kate was sitting in the corner, not saying a word. Wilbur looked at her thoughtfully. He didn't see his mother wink at Kate. He knew, though, that Kate must have told their mother how badly he and Orv needed money. But he also knew that his mother and Kate wanted that to be a secret between them, so he didn't say anything about it.

"Orv," he said, "you go to Cincinnati tomorrow. Now let's figure out what we need. If we can buy in quantity, we can get things cheaper."

"Let's use the kitchen table," Orv said, and they grabbed paper and pencils and ran to the kitchen. It was midnight before they finished writing down just what they would need.

The next day Orville went to all of the bicycle factories in Cincinnati, inspecting their bikes and their spare parts. He ordered tires from one factory, pedals from another, wheels from a third. Then he hurried home.

When the spare parts arrived, the Wright brothers worked as they'd never worked before. Day after day they were in their shop until midnight, tearing apart old bikes and then rebuilding them.

At that time the bicycles that were sold by the big companies cost a hundred dollars. Why were they so expensive? Well, "mass production" had not yet come into existence. Everything had to be made by hand, and that took a long time. Wilbur and Orville could undersell the big companies because they had no payroll. They didn't even pay themselves a salary. They just divided the profits three ways and then bought more old bikes and more spare parts with their profits.

When they sold a Wright Flier, they said they would give free service for a year. In other words, if something went wrong with the bike during the first year, the owner had only to bring it back to the shop on West Third Street and Will or Orv Wright would fix it at no cost. The owners of a Columbia or a Pope, on the other hand, were not so well off. The factories making those bikes were at least three or four hundred miles away; and if the

Wright brothers or anyone else fixed the bikes there was naturally a charge. So the offer of free service drew many customers.

Soon Will and Orv had so many orders for new bikes that they had to hire a couple of boys to help them. They were making plenty of money now, but oddly enough, they weren't satisfied.

The truth is that one of the qualities they both had was curiosity. They had been curious about bicycles. It had been an exciting adventure to fix a broken-down old bike or to assemble a new one out of lots of junk and a few new parts. But after they'd done it a hundred times, they found they weren't curious anymore. They had always been like that. Now they wanted to try something different.

Visitors at the shop used to hear a lot of banging out in back. When they investigated they found that Wilbur and Orv were building a wooden shack in the back yard.

"What are you going to use that for?" they'd ask.

Orv would shrug his shoulders and say, "Oh, I don't know. Just to fool around in."

Soon the building was finished. Will and

Orv installed a workbench and a lathe. This place would be completely separate from the shop. They'd just "fool around" in here. Maybe they'd get an idea that would improve their bicycles. They had a big drawing board where they could draw plans, and they had their tools and their workbench.

One day Kate burst into their shack. She was the only one allowed in. Her face was white and there were tears in her eyes.

"Come home," she gasped. "Mother . . ."

That's all they had to hear. They dropped everything and rushed home. They knew their mother hadn't been well for some time. She had lost a lot of weight and she had no appetite. But they hadn't thought there was anything seriously the matter with her. When they reached home they realized they'd been wrong. She had known how sick she was but she had made the doctor promise not to tell her sons. Only she and Kate knew. When the boys reached home their father was just coming out of her room.

He shook his head, and then Will and Orv knew they had lost the best friend they would ever have.

12

Typhoid Fever

Will and Orv didn't do anything the next few years except work. Everyone knew how much they had loved their mother, and everyone was sympathetic. People felt that the two brothers wanted to be left alone, and they were right. Wilbur and Orv never mentioned their mother even to their best friends. They worked and worked and worked. That's all they did. And if they had secret dreams, they kept them to themselves.

On Sundays they'd take long walks. No one else ever knew what they talked about on those walks. Very often they went to the Big Hill to watch the boys flying their kites.

One Sunday eleven-year-old Walter Brookins was among the boys on the hill. He lived near the Wrights and his father had bought one of their bikes for Walter. Walter was flying a homemade kite, and suddenly it took a dive into a tree. There wasn't much left of it when Walter brought it down from the tree.

"You come around to the shop tomorrow," Orv said. "We'll make you a new kite."

They made him a box kite the next day, and of course they had to try it out themselves. Now they went to the Big Hill more often, making kites for the boys and flying them, too. Some people shook their heads. One said, "Seems silly to me. Why, they're grown men now and there they are, flying kites like a couple of kids."

But Wilbur and Orville were doing more than just "flying kites." They watched the kites they had made in order to study what happened when a strong wind came up. Once they had a box kite about half a mile up in the air. Suddenly it began to rain fiercely, and the wind blew hard, but the Wrights noticed that their kite was flying steadily and evenly.

"Funny thing about the wind," Will said. "Down here it's blowing almost a storm; up there where the kite is there's hardly any wind."

"We ought to learn more about wind and air currents," Orville said. "But let's call it a day, Will. I feel tired."

Wilbur looked at Orville sharply. It wasn't like Orv to admit to being tired. He noticed that Orville's face was flushed. Will called, "Hey, Walter, take care of this kite for us," and Walter Brookins was glad to do that.

A half-hour later Orville was home in bed and the doctor was examining him.

"I guess I caught a cold, Doctor," Orville muttered.

"I guess you have, Orv," the doctor said dryly. "You're going to stay in bed awhile. And I'm going to get a nurse to take care of you."

"I'll take care of Orv," Kate said. "He won't need a nurse."

"You'll take care of him during the daytime," the doctor said. "I'm going to get a night nurse, too."

"Just for a little cold?" Orville was half-asleep, but he managed to say that.

"This isn't a little cold, Kate," the doctor said. "This is typhoid fever."

Typhoid fever! Wilbur's face turned white. Kate was pale, too, but she said calmly, "We'll help him to get well."

"How did he catch it?" Will asked shakily.

"Nobody knows how you catch it," the doctor said sorrowfully. "And even we doctors aren't positive how to cure it. But his temperature is high. We must bring it down. Will, I'll write out a prescription. You hurry to the drugstore and have it filled. Kate, set a big pot of water up next to Orv's bed. Put a piece of ice in it. Then get a cloth and keep bathing Orv's forehead. We have to make his temperature go down."

In those days, most people who had typhoid fever died from it. It was one of the deadliest of all diseases. Doctors didn't know about inoculations then. Today nearly every child in America is vaccinated against smallpox when he goes to school, and most parents have their children inoculated against typhoid fever. Every single soldier in World War II was inoculated against typhoid fever, and very few of them caught the disease. But when Orville contracted it in 1896, doctors hadn't yet learned about vaccinations and inoculations.

Orville was unconscious for nearly two weeks. The doctor had brought a night nurse to the house, but Will and Kate did most of the nursing. They took turns sitting at Orv's bedside, sponging him with cold water. Despite this, his fever kept mounting until it reached 105 degrees.

About half the time Orville was delirious, and he kept mumbling strange things. That is, they were strange to Kate but not to Will. "We flew. We flew," Orville would cry, and Will knew that Orville, in his delirium, was thinking of the time they first coasted down the Big Hill on the sled their mother had helped them make.

Strange phrases like "wind pressure" and "vertical air currents" meant nothing to Kate, but Wilbur knew that Orville was thinking of kites, kites that would carry a man up into the air. They'd talked of such kites on their long Sunday walks, but didn't know enough about how to make them to get beyond talking about it.

Three horrible weeks went by. Kate grew big-eyed and thin from lack of sleep. The doctor came twice a day but there wasn't much he could do. "The fever has to run its course," he'd say almost angrily. He was angry because he felt helpless.

You never hear a doctor say, "This disease has to run its course" today. Today doctors know how to fight many kinds of disease, and they have medicines and drugs to kill the germs that cause the disease. It was different at the turn of the century. Orville kept losing weight. He was nothing but skin and bones; the fever was burning away his flesh.

Then one morning Kate touched his forehead and found that it was cool. She heard a weak voice ask, "How long have I been sick?" And she knew that the worst was over. The fever had run its course. The doctor came hurrying.

"Thank God," he said when he took Orville's temperature. It was almost normal.

"Am I better?" Orville whispered.

"No," the doctor said, smiling. "But you're going to be better. You'll have to stay in bed for at least two months to get back your strength."

"Two months?" Orville protested.

"In about two weeks I'll let you sit up," the doctor promised.

"Can't I even read a book?" Orv asked.

"No," the doctor said sharply.

"I'll read to you, Orv," Will said. "I got some new books. One of them is wonderful. It's by Otto Lilienthal. It's called *Experiments in Soaring.*"

"*Experiments in Soaring,*" Orville repeated, and now his eyes were bright for the first time in weeks. "I read about him in a . . ."

"That's enough, Orv," the doctor said. "You just soar into sleep. Will can read to you tomorrow."

Orville closed his eyes and was sound asleep immediately.

Wilbur walked to the road with the doctor and watched him climb into his buggy.

"This is going to be hard on Orville," the doctor said gravely as he picked up the reins. "He must lie absolutely quiet. Nature has to be given a chance to build him up again and give him back his strength. You've got to keep him interested so he won't get restless."

"I'll keep him interested," Will promised. "Just wait until he hears what Lilienthal has done. Doctor, he has actually made a kite that carries him up into the air. He has flown!"

"Oh, come now, Wilbur," the doctor said, laughing. "If you don't stop talking like that

I'll begin to think *you're* delirious." Then he cracked his whip and his old horse ambled down the road.

Wilbur stood there for a moment.

"I guess Orv and I had better keep our ideas to ourselves," he said to himself. "Or people will think that we're crazy."

13

Learning Through Reading

It was three days later. Wilbur was reading out loud.

> "When I was a boy I watched the birds gliding. I tried to make kites that would glide like a bird. None of them were successful. Then I realized that the wings of a bird were not flat; they were curved. I made a large kite shaped something like the wing of a bird. I released it from the top of a hill and, sure enough, it glided quite some distance and then it settled easily on the ground."

"That's how Otto Lilienthal began," Wilbur said excitedly. "That's the one thing we never thought of, Orv—making kites that were curved a bit."

"How did you hear about Otto Lilienthal?" Orville asked curiously. He was lying flat on the bed but his eyes were alert. He was so weak that he couldn't raise his hand from the cover, but as he listened to Will reading from *Experiments in Soaring* he felt new strength pouring into him.

"One of the bicycle firms sent us a magazine," Will said. "They sent it because there was a story in it about the new coaster their bike has. The magazine also had a series about the new horseless carriages some people are working on, and it had a story about Otto Lilienthal. At the end of the story it said that anyone who wanted a copy of his book could get it by writing to the Smithsonian Institution in Washington."

"What's the Smithsonian Institution?" Orv asked.

"It's owned by the government, Orv, and a man named Professor Samuel Langley is head of it. I wrote for the book and the professor sent it and also wrote me. He said if we were interested in 'soaring,' he had a number of other books we could have. So I wrote for them and—well, Orville—you have no idea how many men are experimenting with soaring."

"Tell me more about Otto Lilienthal," Orv begged eagerly.

"He seems something like us," said Will, laughing. "First he flew kites, and just like us, he dreamed of a kite that would take him up into the sky. Finally, after trying dozens of kites, he made one that actually did fly. He calls it a glider."

"A glider," Orville repeated.

"He takes off from the top of a hill," Will said, "and then the wind carries him from there out into the valley. He said that he has made flights of almost a minute when the wind was right."

"It all depends on the wind, doesn't it," Orv said.

"What do you mean, Orv?" Will asked.

"I mean you aren't really flying unless you're the boss," Orv said. "Even if you're up in a glider, you're at the mercy of the wind. You have to go where the wind tells you to go.

Wouldn't it be great if you yourself, and not the wind, could say where you wanted to go? By the way, who besides Otto Lilienthal is experimenting with soaring?"

"Well," Wilbur said, "Professor Langley at the Smithsonian Institution is experimenting, and a man named Octave Chanute in Chicago, and another named Hiram Maxim. But Lilienthal, so far as I know, is the only one who actually gets on a glider and flies. The others write about their theories—and maybe they're wonderful theories—but Lilienthal is the first man to soar himself."

"Maybe he makes a drawing, and if the drawing is right the glider will be right." Orville smiled.

"That's exactly what he does," Will said excitedly. "Just as Mother taught us to do. Now you stay quiet and I'll read some more."

Orville lay there all afternoon listening to Will read Lilienthal's book. When Will had finished that, he read a magazine article by Octave Chanute. In the Dayton library he had found a book on the flight of birds, and he read that to Orville, too.

One day a batch of pamphlets arrived from the Smithsonian Institution. They contained more articles on "soaring," as some called it, or "gliding," as others called it. They made exciting reading, and Orville lay there dreaming his dreams that someday would shake the world, but only Wilbur knew what they were. Will had told Orv about what the doctor had said. If a smart man like the doctor thought people who talked about flying were crazy, think how the ordinary man would feel!

"I wish we could make enough money so we could make a glider and do some experimenting far away from here," Orv said. "But when I get out of bed we'll have to knuckle down and get back some of the business that the shop has lost in the past couple of months."

"What shop lost what business?" Will laughed. "Those bike races have kept right on, Orv. And do you know I won three of them in a row while you were sick? Then I quit. Why, we have more orders for bikes than we can fill. And I made a deal with a bike factory that failed. I bought a hundred bike frames from them for almost nothing. Going to pay them back so much a month. I have three of the boys at the shop working now at assembling new bikes. We're all right at the shop, Orv. You just get better and take your time about it."

"All right, Will," Orville said. "Now let's write to Mr. Chanute and some of these others. Just say we're interested in experimenting with gliders and ask them if they can recommend any magazines or books to us."

Within two weeks Orv had a dozen scientific magazines in which there were articles about gliding. They were written for the most part by college professors, inventors, engineers, and scientists. Scientists are probably the most wonderful people in the world. They like to share their knowledge with others. Perhaps a man would find that the only way to launch a glider was against the wind, and that as long as it headed into the wind you could control it to some extent. Being a scientist, he wouldn't keep the knowledge to himself. He'd write an article for a magazine so that everyone would know about it.

Orville began to get magazines like *The Railroad and Engineering Journal.* Now remember, although Will and Orv were then in their twenties, neither had ever graduated from high school. (Thomas Edison, who was then America's most famous inventor, had never graduated from high school either.)

Wilbur and Orv, however, were smart enough to know that to understand the technical terms used in the magazines they were reading, they had to learn about physics and at least the fundamentals of engineering and mechanical drawing. So they borrowed technical books and really studied them.

It took Orville a long time to recover fully from the attack of typhoid fever, but this gave him a chance to study and learn everything that was then known about gliding. At night, when Will came back from the shop, Orville would tell him just what he'd learned during the day.

A whole year passed and now the two had only one ambition: they would build a glider and fly it farther than anyone else had ever done.

"We'll fly yet," Wilbur said grimly.

"You bet we will," the loyal Orv told him.

14

They Make a Glider

It was a year later. Kate finally allowed Orville to go to the shop. That was a happy moment for all three of them. Orville always liked to make things. He knew that the huge amount of reading and studying he and Will had been doing was necessary, but the real joy lay in actually seeing something grow before their eyes.

As he stepped into the shop, Orville felt as if he had returned home. He loved the pleasant smell of wood and oil.

Then Will led him to the shack behind the shop.

Orville blinked when he walked into the

low, one-room wooden building. In one corner was a quantity of rolled-up cloth and in another were several dozen long sticks of light wood.

"I bought this so it would be here when you were ready to go to work," Wilbur said.

"Does anyone know what the cloth and the sticks are for?" Orville asked.

"Only Kate," Will said, smiling.

"I told everybody that you were going camping when you had a chance," said Kate, "and that naturally you had to make a couple of tents."

"Nobody must know," Orville said, "or they'll think we're crazy."

"They even laugh at people who think the motor car will take the place of the horse," Kate said. "Imagine what they would say if they knew that you two were going to fly!"

"*Maybe* we're going to fly," Wilbur corrected her.

"Go on," Kate scoffed. "When you two say you're going to do something, you do it."

"I hope you're right, Kate," Wilbur said seriously. "But we must keep our plans quiet."

And they had plenty of plans. One of the magazines that Orville had sent for had a picture of something brand new—something called a "motor boat." It had been invented by a German, and the picture showed it carrying eleven people on a lake near Württemberg. It was a pretty big boat, but it had a very small engine.

That same week the big Barnum and Bailey Circus came to Dayton and, needless to say, Wilbur and Orville went to see it. They didn't care much about the elephants, the lions, or the clowns, but they became really excited when they saw a horseless carriage for the first time. It looked like a carriage, it was a carriage, but it wasn't pulled by a horse. It was run by an engine, and the circus people called it a motor car. A few years later people would call it an "automobile."

They talked of little else during the following weeks.

"You can run a boat with an engine," Orv would say. "You can run a carriage with an engine. Maybe someday we'll be able to run a glider with an engine."

"That would be a real flying machine,"

Wilbur said, his eyes sparkling. "Then you wouldn't have to go wherever the wind blew you. You could have some kind of rudder on it so that you could steer it—the way a boat is steered."

"Let's start building a flying machine right away," Orv blurted out.

Wilbur laughed. "Hold your horses, Orv," he said. "First we have to build a glider. Then we have to coast in it like Otto Lilienthal did. We have to learn everything we can about gliding or soaring. Then we have to learn everything we can about engines. Then maybe we can put the two together."

The next day in their shack they started to draw plans for their first glider. By now, of course, they had studied everything that Octave Chanute and Otto Lilienthal had written about the different types of gliders, and they had decided that the double-decker glider would be best. (Afterward this would be called a biplane.) Their glider began to grow on the drawing board.

"This has to be right," Wilbur warned, "because a glider costs a lot of money. We can't risk breaking it."

"I'll tell you something, Will," Orv said.

"No matter how right this looks on paper, we can't be sure it's right until we try it out in the air."

"That's true, Orv," Will said.

"Well, we can't try it out around here," Orv went on. "People would laugh at us. And then there are too many hills and trees. Every time we flew our glider we'd probably run it into a tree. We ought to find some place where there is always a steady wind blowing and where there aren't many trees. We need some hills, all right, but we need a place with soft ground, too."

"That's right," Wilbur nodded. "You write to the Smithsonian Institution and ask them where there is such a place."

Orv did write to the Smithsonian Institution, and the kindly Professor Langley sent their letter to the United States Weather Bureau. The Weather Bureau wrote Orv, telling him of several places where there were steady winds and no trees. Orv and Will went over the letter carefully.

"Here's a place called Kitty Hawk, in North Carolina," Orv said.

"Kitty Hawk?" Wilbur repeated. "That's a nice name."

"We'll build a glider here, take it apart, and then go to Kitty Hawk." Orv had it all planned.

"Let's wait until the fall," Will advised. "The bicycle business won't be so good then."

"But let's not tell anyone," Orv said.

"Except Kate," Will told him. "And Father, when he gets back from his trip."

"I mean nobody but them," Orv corrected himself.

They really worked that summer. They were at the shop at six every morning. They didn't want to miss a single customer. But at eight o'clock in the evening they locked the shop and hurried to their shack. Then the real work began. Sometimes they wouldn't get home until midnight, but Kate always had a hot meal ready for them.

"What's the best way to learn how to ride a horse?" Wilbur asked one day.

"Well," Orv said, "you can sit on a fence and watch somebody else try to stay on a horse. You can study the mistakes that person makes and learn why the horse keeps throwing him off. Then when you've found out all the *wrong* ways to ride a horse you'll know the *right* way, and you can get on his back and do it that way."

"That's one way," Wilbur agreed. "That's the way most of the scientists are studying gliders. But most people learn to ride a horse by hopping on his back and actually riding. We'll combine both ways. Our glider is almost ready. We can finish it at Kitty Hawk. Then if it seems all right we'll hop on it and actually ride."

"That suits me, Will," Orv said.

"Now let's find out how to get to this place—Kitty Hawk," Will said.

15

Kitty Hawk

Today you could get on an airplane at Dayton and be at Kitty Hawk in less than two hours. But it took Wilbur and Orv a week to reach the lonely fishing hamlet. Kitty Hawk is about sixty miles from Cape Hatteras, which is one of the stormiest places on the Atlantic Coast. But it is rarely stormy at Kitty Hawk. It is a place of sand dunes and gentle hills and no trees at all.

"This is perfect," Wilbur said. "And best of all, there are scarcely any people here. Nobody will think we're crazy when we start flying our glider."

They had brought a tent with them and

they put it up. Kate had packed a suitcase with jelly and jam and other foods she always canned at home. Will and Orv had brought all of their precious books and pamphlets and all kinds of tools with them, and now they were ready for the big test.

Kitty Hawk, the scene of their test, consisted of nothing but a government weather bureau and a life-saving station, but because of these it had a post office. This was run by Mr. William Tate, and Will and Orv arranged with Mrs. Tate to have their meals with the family.

As they assembled their glider, there was no one to laugh at them but a few seagulls hovering above. The glider was just a big box kite with an upper and a lower wing. Mr. Tate (who only had four or five letters a day to deliver) looked at it curiously, but he didn't laugh. There was something about these two serious-eyed young men that kept a person from laughing. Mr. Tate, in fact, asked if he could help them.

Well, they needed a helper. They had reached the point where they had "studied the way to ride a horse," and now they had to climb on its back and see if they could stay on. One of them would ride the glider, but two others were needed to run ahead and give it a start. This glider had to be pulled along just as a kite was pulled along, until the wind grabbed it and took it up into the air. They tossed a coin and Orville won. He'd be the first rider.

Otto Lilienthal and the other glider experts always sat upright on the lower wing of the gliders. Wilbur remembered the first time his mother had used the expression "wind resistance," and he remembered how fast his sled had gone when he had lain on it. And of course he remembered how fast Orville had gone on his bike when he had lowered the handlebars and leaned over to "get under the wind."

"Lie down on the wing, Orv," Will said. "That'll reduce the wind resistance."

Orv nodded and took his place. The glider was nestled on top of a sand dune. Wilbur and Mr. Tate stood on either side of it. Wilbur had attached strong cords to each side of the glider, and he and Mr. Tate grabbed the loose ends.

"We'll pull the glider downhill," Will explained to Mr. Tate. "And then . . . well

. . . maybe it'll go up into the air. Ready? One . . . two . . . three . . . GO!"

They trotted down the sand dune, pulling the light glider along. Nothing happened. They ran now faster and faster, and suddenly there was a yell from Orville.

"I'm flying," he cried and, sure enough, the glider was about five feet off the ground. It rose to eight feet, and now Wilbur and Mr. Tate dropped the cords they'd been holding. The glider went beautifully for about a hundred feet—and then a gust of wind took it and almost turned it over. A down draft then sent the glider crashing to the ground. Orv wasn't hurt, but the glider was. But the Wrights didn't care.

"We built a kite that took us into the air!" Orv cried with excitement.

"Now let's fix it and try again," Wilbur said.

Mr. Tate noticed that the cloth was ripped in several places. "Can either of you young men run a sewing machine?" he asked.

"Why sure, Mr. Tate," Orv said.

"Well, Mrs. Tate has a nice new sewing machine she'll be glad to let you borrow," Mr. Tate said. "It'd be a lot quicker than sewing up those . . . those wings . . . by hand."

Wings? Even Mr. Tate was using the word. Orv had flown on wings. Let others call it a big box kite or even a glider. He knew that he had flown on wings. He'd only flown for about ten seconds, but he had flown.

The next day it was Wilbur's turn. He stayed up a little longer. Every day now the Wrights tried out their glider. Whichever one was on the ground took notes of what was happening. They found out a great many things. They discovered that if the wind was right, they could actually go about ten miles an hour. They had always believed that balance was the most important thing in kite flying, or, for that matter, in any kind of flying. And their glider had no balance. Whenever a gust of wind hit it, the glider would either turn halfway over or plummet to the ground.

"When the right side of the glider dips, try to shift over to the left side," Wilbur said thoughtfully. "That might balance it."

On their next flight Orv tried that, but it didn't work very well. Then, too, they could not steer their glider. As Will had once said, a glider was at the mercy of the winds.

Every night after dinner at Mrs. Tate's the Wrights would sit around her kitchen table talking about the mistakes that had been made that day. They wrote them all down. The cloth they had been using was called "sateen" (almost like silk). They felt that it "leaked" air. They'd have to find some cloth that was more airtight. And somehow or other they'd have to find a way to balance and steer the glider.

"Let's make a rudder like the one we made for our sled years ago," Orv suggested, and Will thought that a good idea.

"We might try a horizontal rudder, though," Orv said. "One that is parallel to the ground. That might make us go up or down. We'll make it so we can adjust it. Tip it one way, we go up. Tip it another, we go down."

Within three days they had built a rudder. But they attached it to the front of the glider, not the back. There was a good reason for that. The person on the glider had to raise or lower the rudder, and if it was in back of him he wouldn't have been able to get at it.

Wilbur named it the "front elevating rudder." (Ask a pilot what a front elevating rudder is and he'll point it out to you.)

It was Will's turn to fly now, and again Mr. Tate was on hand to help. The winds were stronger than they had been, for it was November now, and winter was approaching. The glider lifted easily into the air. It rose to fifteen feet and then Wilbur tried the rudder. He pulled the two cords that raised the front of it and immediately the glider zoomed up at least another fifteen feet. Then he pulled the two cords again and the glider nosed down. It nosed down fast. Will tried to yank the cords to raise the rudder, but one of them broke and the glider nose-dived right into a sand dune.

Orv had a sinking feeling as he ran to where the glider and Wilbur lay all mixed up with the sand. But Wilbur wasn't even hurt. He was just stunned a little, and he was smiling.

"We did it!" he cried out. "We made it go up and then down. The wind wasn't the boss."

"But look at the glider," Orv said in dismay. "It's completely wrecked."

"We can build another one, Orv," Will said. "And a better one. Mr. Tate, maybe you can use the cloth."

"Mrs. Tate could use it to make our little girl a dress," Mr. Tate said with a smile.

"We're going to pack up and go home," Will said. "But we'll be back next year."

They did pack up, and the day they left for home the Tates' little daughter came to see them. She was wearing a very pretty dress. She never knew that she was wearing part of the most important glider ever made—the first glider that went up or down at the will of the pilot. It was the first glider that had conquered the air.

16

Improving the Glider

"Where've you two been?" a customer asked the Wright brothers on their return.

"We've been camping," Wilbur said, and that was no lie. They had been camping out on the sand dunes at Kitty Hawk. They told only Kate and their father the whole story of what had happened. They had done two things that nobody in the world had ever done before. They had flown in a glider with the pilot lying on the lower wing, and they had built a rudder that made the glider go up or down. They were only two bicycle mechanics to the people in Dayton, but they had done something that none of the great scientists and engineers had ever done.

Over in England, Hiram Maxim was experimenting with "flying machines" and the English government backed him with money and materials. But he had never actually been up in a glider. He made models and sent them up into the air by themselves. He wrote articles about how these models acted in the air.

"You can only learn to ride a horse by getting on his back and riding," Wilbur said, after reading an article by Maxim.

"Same with a bike," Orv said. "You have to take a few spills before you get the knack of it."

They had read more articles by Octave Chanute of Chicago. He didn't just make models; he made gliders and he flew them himself, even though he was about sixty years old. Will and Orv decided to write and tell him what had happened at Kitty Hawk. Chanute was an engineer and a scientist; when he read the Wrights' letter he must have received a shock. These two obscure bicycle mechanics had done something that Otto Lilienthal had never done; that he himself had never done. He wrote and congratulated them, and he told them some new facts that he had learned about the art of gliding.

Will and Orv devoured everything that Mr. Chanute sent them. Then they went back to work. A glider could be made to go up or down. How could it be made to go to the right or to the left? Will and Orv watched birds again as they swooped and turned. A bird had a great advantage over a glider. A bird could raise or lower his wings at will. When a bird turned in flight, one wing was higher than the other. Will and Orv discussed adjustable wings that could be raised or lowered, but that didn't seem practical.

Then there was still the question of balance. Shifting one's own weight to the right or left just didn't make sense.

"I wonder," Orv said one day, "if a second rudder would help the balance—a vertical rudder."

"It might," Wilbur said. "Next time we go to Kitty Hawk we'll try it. Meanwhile, let's put it down on the drawing board."

Should the vertical rudder be in front or in back? The Wrights thought they'd try it at the back of the glider. Less wind resistance. But why not put the horizontal rudder there, too? The odd-looking "tail" of the glider began to take form. (The next time you see an airplane, notice the tail. You'll see both a vertical and a horizontal rudder.)

"Our next glider must be bigger," Wilbur said. "The more wing surface, the longer it will stay up."

"And the higher it will go," Orv added.

"And the more chances of your being killed," Kate broke in. Kate was teaching in a high school now, but she still took care of the house and she was still the only one with whom they discussed all their plans.

"We'll be careful, Kate," Orv promised, smiling.

"Otto Lilienthal was careful and he was killed," she pointed out.

Wilbur and Orv knew that the higher one soared the more dangerous it was, but this was a risk they had to take.

Twice more they made the long trip to Kitty Hawk. The glider they had now was stronger than the first one. But would the vertical rudder work? It worked pretty well. They made one "flight" of three hundred feet which they felt to be a record, but they didn't tell anyone. Only Mr. Tate and the seagulls knew about it. The new glider had balance. It didn't wobble very much.

"If we made that vertical rudder adjustable, like the rudder of a sailboat, maybe it would steer our glider," Orv suggested. That wasn't much of a job for two expert mechanics, and they found it worked fairly well. Best of all, the combination of a vertical and a horizontal rudder made their glider safer than any other ever built. It didn't take sudden nose dives or turn over in mid-air. It was steady.

"We have to practice every day," Wilbur said. "We have to get the feel of the glider, the way we used to get the feel of a new bike."

All day long they took turns gliding. Two of the men at the life-saving station had sons, and the youngsters were only too glad to help launch the glider. Both Will and Orv began to get the feel of it. They found they could turn the glider, they could zoom up or glide downward. Instead of ropes they used piano wire to change the direction of the two rudders, and they now used levers to pull the wires.

They made their longest flight on this third trip to Kitty Hawk—622 feet. The glider had stayed in the air for twenty-six seconds. If they could stay aloft for twenty-six seconds, why not twice or three times that long? They found a higher sand dune about two miles away and took off from there. Up to now they hadn't really tried for altitude. They were sensible enough to know that a fall from a hundred feet would be fatal; a fall from twenty feet would only shake one up a bit. But now they decided that they had pretty good control of their glider.

Orv was at the controls one day. As the glider took off, an "up" current lifted it to two hundred feet. That was an amazing height, and Orv must have felt a bit uncomfortable looking down. But he also found that the glider was even easier to control at that height. So he tilted the horizontal rudder and the glider zoomed up another fifty feet. Then the wind died down and the glider came down to earth. Orv had been up for fifty seconds. Not even Otto Lilienthal had ever stayed aloft that long.

"There are plenty of improvements we can make," Orv said that night. "Maybe we should have a double-decker horizontal rudder. I think that will keep us up longer."

"I have some other ideas, too, Orv," Will said. "But I think we can work them out better at home."

Once again they packed and headed back for Dayton.

17

The Wright Engine

The next few years were exciting ones. Mr. Chanute came to see the Wrights and he told them of experiments he had been making. He told of his first glider—it had five decks. Then he'd tried one with three wings. Both gliders had been too heavy. Like Wilbur and Orv, he had finally decided that a biplane with two wings, one above the other, was the only answer. But although he had built more than two hundred gliders, he had never made one as strong as the one the two bicycle mechanics from Dayton had made.

The Wright brothers admired Chanute a great deal. Building gliders had been his hobby for thirty years, but he had never actually flown in one until he was past sixty. Now, nearing seventy, he still "flew."

"But you two are the only ones ready to add power to the glider and really make a successful flying machine," Mr. Chanute said enthusiastically. "I want to help you. Let me finance you so you can give up your bicycle shop and spend all of your time experimenting."

Wilbur smiled and shook his head. "We've never borrowed any money, except from our mother," he said, "and we're not going to start now."

They kept on studying engines. They needed an engine powerful enough to make their glider go against the wind, yet light enough to enable the glider to get into the air.

In Washington, Professor Langley had announced that he had made a flying machine. He had, too. The only trouble with it was that he couldn't get it into the air. He tried to launch it, but the heavy flying machine just wouldn't rise from the ground.

In France, a young man named Santos-Dumont had attached an engine to a balloon and had actually flown. This was the first "blimp," but it went very slowly and couldn't make much headway against the wind. Besides, it was a "lighter-than-air" experiment. The Wright brothers were interested only in making "heavier-than-air" flying machines.

They still kept their plans secret. In 1900, people laughed at anyone who said that man could fly. Even the scientists who should have known better ridiculed the idea, and one of them wrote a magazine article saying, "Man will not fly for a thousand years." Everyone was laughing at poor Professor Langley in Washington.

Mr. Chanute was one of the few who didn't laugh. He knew that the two young men from Dayton were touched with genius. Although they were completely self-taught, they knew more about wind pressure and air resistance and the strength of the material that went into a glider than anyone else alive. And they were the two best pilots in the world. They had made more than a thousand flights in their glider. They "had the feel of it."

Kitty Hawk was too far away, so the Wrights continued their experiments in a cow pasture near Dayton. Every time one of them took off in the glider he took along a sack of sand. They found the glider would stay aloft with the weight of one man—plus a hundred-pound sack of sand. But the automobile engines of the day weighed at least three hundred pounds. They couldn't use an automobile engine to power their glider; it would just be too heavy.

They kept on making small improvements in their glider, making it stronger but lighter, and finally found that the glider would carry a sack weighing nearly two hundred pounds. Now if they could buy a good engine that weighed only two hundred pounds, they felt they would really be able to fly.

But no one in the world was building such an engine.

"We'll build one ourselves," Orv said.

"Now that I think of it," and Wilbur smiled, "nobody ever really built anything for us."

They began to construct an engine in the wooden shack in back of the store. Basically it was much like the airplane engine of today. It operated by gasoline; it had a carburetor and spark plugs, but of course it had no self-starter. Sometimes at night people walking along the street would be startled to hear what sounded like machine-gun fire coming from the shack behind the Wright Cycle Company.

"Those crazy Wright brothers are at it again," they'd say with a laugh.

Word got around that the two brothers were experimenting with an engine to be attached to a bicycle, and that explained the sharp explosions that came from the wooden shack. It may be that Kate started the story.

The engine began to take final shape. Will and Orv had a helper now, faithful Charley Taylor, a good mechanic. Charley took care of the shop when the Wright brothers were busy, and at night he helped them in the wooden shack. Only Charley and Kate were allowed in this secret workroom.

It was easy to build an engine that was powerful enough. The difficult thing was to make the engine light enough. The engine case was always one of the heaviest parts of a motor. It was made of cast iron.

"If we made this out of aluminum it would be a lot lighter," Orv said one day.

"But would it be strong enough?" Wilbur asked.

"All we can do is try it," Orv said, and they did. It proved to be light and strong. The engine had four cylinders and eight horsepower. (During World War II, fighter-plane engines had 1500 horsepower.) Oddly enough, even now the strength of engines is measured by horsepower.

In the early days every farmer knew just how big a load one horse could pull. The men who made the early engines would say, "This engine can pull as big a load as four horses could pull," so gradually they began to call such an engine a "four-horsepower engine." Even today, if an engine has a "thousand horsepower," it means that it can pull a load as heavy as a thousand horses, all pulling at once, could move.

The Wright brothers' little eight-horsepower engine weighed just two hundred pounds. When it was finished, Will and Orv carved two propellers out of spruce logs.

"Remember that little toy Father gave us years ago?" Orv said.

"The helicopter? Sure, I remember," and Wilbur laughed. "Funny—we're really making a big toy with two propellers that move in opposite directions, just as they did on that toy."

"I remember it, too," Kate said soberly. "And I remember that it smashed into a tree and was broken to bits."

"There are no trees at Kitty Hawk," Wilbur reminded her.

"And that's where we are going to fly," Orv said.

18

The Flying Machine

Kitty Hawk hadn't changed much. William Tate was a little older but no busier than he had been on the Wright brothers' first visit. He helped them build a shed to protect their glider and its engine from the storms that occasionally swept over the sand dunes. Then Will and Orv gave him the job of bringing firewood every morning. They paid him a dollar a day for that.

All day long they worked on their glider and their engine. It was a funny-looking thing, and when the men from the life-saving station walked over to look at it they shook their heads.

"You really going to make this thing fly?" one of them asked Wilbur.

"Maybe, maybe," Will said.

"How long you been working on this?" another asked.

"All our lives," Orville said, and that was the truth.

Their first flying machine—the word airplane wasn't used then—didn't have wheels. It had skids (something like skis). Will and Orv built two wooden tracks and laid them out on the sand. They would launch their flying machine from this track. They tested the engine again and again. It made a lot of noise and it shook the whole glider, but it was well fastened to the lower wing and it would not fly off. At least, they hoped it wouldn't.

"I think we can try it today," Will said casually on the morning of December 17, 1903. Will probably didn't realize that forever and ever, boys and girls in school would learn that date.

"We're as ready as we ever will be," Orv said just as casually.

Outwardly they were calm, but they were human, and you can be sure that they were excited inside. They tossed a coin to decide which one would try the machine first. Orv won.

"I'm going to fly today," Orv whispered to himself. "I'm going to be the first man in the world to fly."

There were only five people out near the lonely sand dune to watch the flying machine try to get into the air, and not one of them thought it could do it. One of the five was a sixteen-year-old boy named Johnny Moore, whose father was a fisherman. They started up the engine. Orv climbed onto the lower wing. Wilbur steadied the glider, which was vibrating terrifically.

"You ready, Orv?" Wilbur shouted.

"All set," Orv yelled back.

"Let her go," Wilbur cried, and Orv released the lever that made the propellers "bite" into the air. The glider started to move along the track slowly . . . a bit quicker . . . and then just as it reached the end of the track, the front of the glider rose up, the rest followed, and the flying machine was in the air. It rose to ten feet. It was flying. It sped along in the air. Wilbur, usually calm, was trembling with joy. Orville was actually flying. The flying machine went a hundred and twenty feet and then it glided down gracefully to the sand.

Orville tumbled out of the first machine that had ever really flown.

"We did it, Will," he said, his voice shaky.

"We can fly," Wilbur said with awe. "We can fly."

"How long was I up?" Orv asked.

"Twelve seconds," Will said. "Now let me try it."

Wilbur flew a hundred and seventy-five feet and then let the machine come down. Orville tried again and came down after about fifteen seconds.

"Will, see how far you can fly it," Orville suggested when Wilbur took his position to try again. Will nodded. Once again the flying machine was launched. It rose to about twenty feet and then Wilbur leveled it off. Looking down, he saw the sand dunes flying past him. The flying machine kept on and on. This was a real flight. Two startled seagulls flew alongside, screaming shrilly. What new kind of bird was this? When Wilbur had flown eight hundred and fifty-two feet, a downward draft of air forced the flying machine to land.

"You were up there fifty-nine seconds," Orv shouted as Wilbur climbed down from the lower wing.

"Next time we'll stay up fifty-nine minutes," Wilbur said with a laugh.

"Let's send a telegram to Father," Orv said.

The four men and the sixteen-year-old boy who had watched the first flight of an airplane came running up to shake hands with the two brothers. Even now they could hardly believe their eyes. They had seen a heavy, ungainly looking glider with a heavy engine actually rise from the ground and fly. No one else in history had ever seen anything like this before.

Wilbur and Orville hurried to send a telegram to their father and to Kate. Back home, the bishop and his daughter read the telegram with shining eyes. They ran to the shop to tell Charley Taylor about it. He wasn't a bit excited.

"Knew they'd do it all along," he said calmly.

A week later Wilbur and Orville came home. There was no brass band to meet them. There were no newspaper men at the station. Bishop Wright and Kate were the only ones to welcome them.

"We flew, Kate," Orv said happily.

"They don't believe it," Kate said angrily.

"Who doesn't believe it?" Will asked.

"The newspapers, the people, even the neighbors," Kate said bitterly.

"First they think we're crazy," Orv said. "Now they think we're liars."

"Don't worry, boys," their father said. "I once told you that God had big plans for you two. I was right. No one can interfere with his plans, my sons. He gave you something special that allowed you to be the first two men in history to fly. Let people laugh."

"We'll show them," Orv said grimly.

19

Airplane in a Cow Pasture

Torrence Huffman, president of a Dayton bank, owned an eighty-acre cow pasture outside the town. Will and Orv asked him if they could use the pasture.

"Somebody said you two have been experimenting with flying machines." Mr. Huffman smiled. "Is that right?"

"That's right," Wilbur said.

"Go ahead, boys, use the field," Mr. Huffman said, "but don't kill any of my cows."

The brothers had decided to build a brand-new flying machine with a sixteen-horsepower engine. They worked hard at it and now, embittered by the attitude of their neighbors, they seldom saw anyone but Charley Taylor and their sister, Kate. When they walked along the street, people winked at each other as if to say, "They're the ones who said they flew." Will and Orv ignored the winks and the scorn, but it hurt them to know that their own neighbors thought they had lied.

Mr. Chanute knew they hadn't lied. He went to Paris and made a speech about the flight at Kitty Hawk, and everyone in France became excited about the flying machine the Wright brothers had built. The Wrights were famous in France, and then in Germany and England, but not in Dayton.

"Why don't they stick to their bicycle shop?" the people said, but the two brothers went right on working. They brought their new flying machine to the cow pasture. But they tried it out only early in the morning. Nobody was going to have a chance to laugh at them. Their new flying machine stayed up longer than the Kitty Hawk machine.

Then one day Wilbur actually circled the field. The new flying machine could steer. Miracles were happening at this cow pasture every day, but no one saw them except for a few cows down at the far end of the pasture. A few days later Orv circled the field three times—a distance of three miles.

One day Will and Orv asked their father and Kate to go to the cow pasture with them.

"Be sure and bring your watch, Father," Will said.

Kate and Bishop Wright stood beside the flying machine.

"I want you to time this flight," Wilbur said. "I've filled the gasoline tank. Now, Orv, take her up."

Orv took her up. The flying machine almost disappeared in the distance, and then it turned and came back. Orv flew over his father's head and waved to him. Then he made a large circle around the field. Bishop Wright kept one eye on his watch. The minutes passed. Fifteen . . . twenty . . . thirty.

"He's been up there half an hour, Will!" Bishop Wright said excitedly.

Finally the flying machine swooped to a gentle landing.

"Thirty-nine minutes!" Bishop Wright gasped.

"I only came down because I ran out of gasoline," Orv explained.

"We can stay up almost as long as we want," Wilbur said. "But we wanted you to see our airplane in action."

"Airplane? That's a good name for it," the Bishop said.

Bishop Wright told a few people what he had seen at the cow pasture. They believed him, and now they were willing to believe Wilbur and Orville. People hurried to the bicycle shop to congratulate them, but the two brothers were too busy to see them.

"Where were they when we came back from Kitty Hawk?" Will asked bitterly.

"Well, we've gotten along without them all these years," Orv said. "We can still get along without them."

One week two important men arrived in Dayton. One was French; the other was English. Each wanted to buy the Wright brothers' airplane. Each wanted to pay a huge sum for the exclusive rights to it so that only his country could make it.

"The Germans will make war on us one day," the Frenchman said excitedly, "and with this flying machine we can beat them easily. We can fly over their armies and drop dynamite on them."

"We too fear Germany," the Englishman said, "and we are willing to pay you anything you want for the right to make your airplane."

"But we are Americans," Wilbur said. "If we give the airplane to anyone it will be to our own army."

"But Monsieur Wright, if you will forgive me," the Frenchman said, "your own army has already refused it. Your own army is not interested."

Wilbur was startled. It is true that he and Orv had written to the army authorities in Washington, and that the army hadn't been interested. But neither he nor Orv had told anybody about this.

"Nevertheless," Wilbur said now, "we are Americans, and someday perhaps our army will be interested."

The two polite gentlemen from abroad bowed, looked regretful, and left.

"I guess we'd better give a real demonstratio , Will said. "I don't blame our army authorities for not being enthusiastic. They've never seen our plane fly."

"All right, Will, we'll give them something to think about," Orv said.

20

Fame and Success

Theodore Roosevelt was President of the United States then. Although he is remembered as a man of action, he was also a great reader, and one day he picked up a copy of the *Scientific American*. There was an article in it about the Wright brothers and their flying machine.

"Get hold of these two young men," President Roosevelt told his Secretary of War, "and have them give an exhibition. Maybe they have something in that flying machine."

One day a dignified colonel arrived in Dayton. He went to see the Wright brothers.

Would they be so good as to honor a request by the President of the United States?

"Frankly, gentlemen," the colonel said, "we in the army don't think the flying machine has any future, but the President has ordered us to get in touch with you. Will you give a demonstration of your machine?"

"You bet we will," Orville said, and Wilbur nodded vigorously.

"Of course we will see that it is held in secret," the colonel said, smiling.

"Why?" Wilbur asked.

"Well, in case things go wrong. . . . I mean if it doesn't get off the ground. . . ." The colonel faltered. "We don't want you gentlemen to be humiliated."

"Don't worry about us, Colonel," and Orv laughed. "Ask a thousand, ask a million people to the demonstration. We don't care."

A huge crowd assembled at Fort Myer, Virginia, the place the army had picked out for the test. The Secretary of War was there. A dozen generals and at least fifty reporters were present. Nobody really believed that the queer-looking machine could actually fly. Did it fly? Orville took it up and circled the field for one hour. When he landed the crowd went wild with enthusiasm. Even generals with three stars on their shoulders swarmed all over the two calm, unexcited brothers.

"I'd give anything to ride with you in that flying machine," a young lieutenant said. Orville looked at him. The young soldier's eyes were shining. He was Lieutenant Fred Lahm.

"Well, come on, Lieutenant," Orville said. "Climb up in back of me and hang on. . . . Clear the crowd away, please."

The crowd fell back. Orv took off easily with the lieutenant hanging on. They circled the field three times and then landed. The crowd was almost hysterical. It had seen a miracle happen. The generals were thoughtful. This airplane could carry a 180-pound passenger in addition to its pilot. That meant it could carry a 180-pound bomb. Perhaps it could carry more than one bomb.

"Have you sold the rights to this plane to any foreign government?" a general asked.

"We're Americans, General," Orv said simply.

The general shook his hand and said, "Will you have time to see the Secretary of War tomorrow?" The two brothers nodded.

The next morning they woke to find themselves famous. Every newspaper in the country had headlines about their flight. They were the most famous men in the world now. There were big crowds outside the War Department building when they went to see the Secretary of War.

"You've done a great thing, young men," the Secretary of War said, shaking hands with them. "The first men in history to fly. Tell me, can you build larger airplanes than the one you showed us yesterday?"

"It's just a matter of power," Orville said. "If we make stronger, more powerful engines, we can fly bigger airplanes."

"If the power is there, we can make a kitchen table fly," Wilbur said.

"I'm sure you can," the Secretary said. "We want you to build airplanes for our army. Will you?"

"Of course we will," Orv said, and Wilbur added, a bit embarrassed, "I hate to mention it, Mr. Secretary, but . . . we have no money. We spent our last cent to finish the plane we showed you yesterday."

"You'll never need money again." The Secretary smiled. "We'll give you all the money you need. Can you build an airplane that will go forty miles an hour?"

"You name the speed you want," Orv said. "We'll build it to your specifications."

"May we make them in Dayton?" Will said. "That's our home town."

"Of course you may," the Secretary of War said. "When are you planning to return?"

"On the midnight train," Will told him.

"That'll give you time to accept a dinner invitation," the Secretary said, smiling. "The President of the United States has asked me to extend an invitation to dinner tonight. Can you make it?"

Wilbur looked at Orville. Orville looked at Wilbur.

Orville winked at Wilbur. "I think we can make it," he said gravely.

And then the two boys who had learned to fly walked out of the office, arm in arm.

About the Author

Quentin Reynolds was one of the most famous war correspondents during World War II. Born in the Bronx, he grew up in Brooklyn. The author attended Brown University and won the school's heavyweight boxing championship.

As a reporter for the International News Service, he was the first journalist to see and report on the Nazi concentration camps in Hitler's Germany. Mr. Reynolds' next job was as associate editor for *Collier's* magazine. During his fifteen years with *Collier's*, he wrote close to 400 articles—covering World War II from the heart of war-torn France and

Germany. His broadcasts over British radio made him an international celebrity and won praise from Winston Churchill. The author's work took him around the world and brought him into contact with political leaders, sports heroes, and entertainers.

Mr. Reynolds wrote many books for adults, including the best-seller *The Wounded Don't Cry;* and five Landmark books for young readers, among them *Custer's Last Stand, The Life of St. Patrick*, and *The Battle of Britain.*

Relive history!

Turn the page for more great books . . .

Landmark Books® Grades 6 and Up

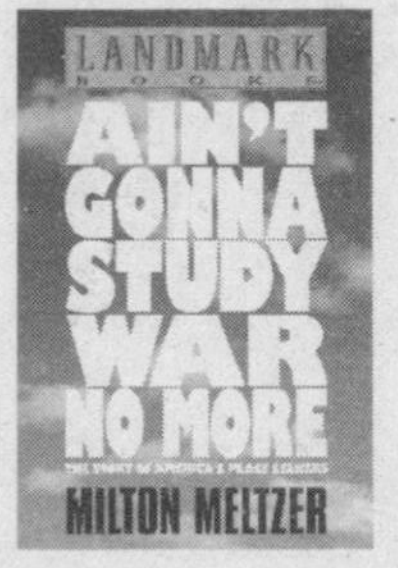

Landmark Books® Grades 4 and Up

Landmark Books® Grades 2 and Up